Shoes on the Highway

SHOES ON THE HIGHWAY

Using Visual and Audio Cues to Inspire Student Playwrights

Maureen Brady Johnson

HEINEMANN ■ Portsmouth, NH

Heinemann
A division of Reed Elsevier Inc.
361 Hanover Street
Portsmouth, NH 03801–3912
www.heinemanndrama.com

Offices and agents throughout the world

The author and publisher wish to thank those who have generously given permission to reprint borrowed material:

Excerpts from "Shoes on the Highway" by Maureen Johnson from *Teaching Theatre Journal* (vol. 14, no 3), Spring 2003. Reprinted by permission.

Library of Congress Cataloging-in-Publication Data
Johnson, Maureen Brady.
Shoes on the highway : using visual and audio cues to inspire student playwrights / Maureen Brady Johnson.
p. cm.
ISBN 0-325-00753-5 (alk. paper)
1. Playwriting. 2. Plots (Drama, novel, etc.). 3. Creation (Literary, artistic, etc.). I. Title.
PN1661.J64 2005
808.2—dc22 2005000320

Editor: Lisa A. Barnett
Production: Elizabeth Valway
Typesetter: Reuben Kantor, QEP Design
Appendix photography: Allison Marie Johnson and Maureen Brady Johnson
Cover photography: Maureen Brady Johnson
Cover design: Night & Day Design
Manufacturing: Louise Richardson

Printed in the United States of America on acid-free paper
09 08 07 06 05 VP 1 2 3 4 5

To my husband, Mark, who stopped the car.

To my daughter, Allison, my co-photographer of shoes.

To my family; Juliet, Sean, Erin and her husband, Josh,
who never thought I was crazy.

And to all the weird circumstances that leave shoes on the highway.

Contents

Foreword

August, 2004. I'm sprawled across an Adirondack chair on the front porch of a beautiful inn in Provincetown, Massachusetts. No matter where I look, I just can't see anything more lazy than me on the landscape. I'm so mellow and lethargic I can barely lift the glass of bourbon to my lips, and yet somehow, some way, it finds its way there. I take my sip, crank down in my chair, throw my legs up on the banister and tilt my head back. And that's when I see it: A single, black stiletto shoe—easily a size eleven, maybe twelve if I could measure it—hanging on a telephone wire by its heel thirty feet over my head. I squint. Is it really a shoe or an overgrown crow on that wire? Nope. No movement; must be a shoe. Not trusting my eyes, and having lost measure of the bourbon in my glass, I lift up from the chair, walk the yard and look up: yep, that's a shoe as sure as I'm standing there. What the heck?

How did that get there? Who does it belong to? A small woman with large feet? A large woman with proportional feet? A drag queen? And where do you get a shoe like that? Who sells a size-twelve stiletto? How long has it been there? Have I been here for the whole month of August and am just now noticing it? Where's the other shoe? Does the owner even know it's there, or was she hitting their bourbon at the time of launch? Is someone still wearing the surviving shoe, gimping around Provincetown—up, down, up, down, up, down? Did it match the outfit? Was it daring footwear, or sensible? Was it a punctuation mark on an already sassy ensemble? Was the pair expensive? Did the owner try to rescue it and look like an idiot while doing so? Am I looking at the subject of someone's dinner-party story for decades to come? Why hasn't the wind blown it down? Am I the first to see this? Am I the last to see this? Is it my own private discovery? Could I get away with claiming that I threw it up there for some inexplicable reason? Will I be crushed when someone says, "Puuuuhlease, it's been there for three years"? A hundred more questions race through my mind as I take great delight in solving the mystery of the hanging shoe with one outrageous possible scenario after another.

All this—for a shoe. Then my housemates retreat to the front porch, discover the object of my attention and a whole other round of questions and positions are thrown out for consideration. Fascinating. Seven reasonably intelligent adults sat around talking about that shoe for a full fifteen minutes, laughing, joking, trying to top one another with a better explanation of the simple questions of how and why? Why indeed?

Maureen Brady Johnson explores the phenomenon of story-building from found objects in this highly imaginative collection of writing exercises for playwrights. Using a physical object as a jumping-off point (an old diary, a coffee mug, sea shells, garden gloves, a tattered coat, shoes on a highway, words painted on a rock, etc.), she challenges her playwrights to answer, "What is the story behind this shoe, outfit, song, keychain . . . ?" and then encourages them to make connections and associations between what may appear to be disparate stimuli, that is "How did this everyday object come to be in this odd place?" (like my Provincetown stiletto hanging on the high wire!).

Any good teacher of playwriting or dramaturgy knows that the creative process is best served when the writer is stimulated with questions that beget more questions, which the dramatist must answer in dramatic form. From these questions (and their answers), the real seeds of story, character, and conflict emerge. *Shoes on the Highway* emulates something that good writers and artists do naturally: link the seemingly unassociated through a vivid imagination.

Look, I've been teaching playwriting for almost twenty-five years. I'm always looking for new ways to stimulate not only my students but my own creative imagination. If playwriting should be equal parts fun, stimulation, challenge, and reward, shouldn't teaching the craft of playwriting be equally so?

If this shoe fits, I'm wearing it, and I think it does.

Gary Garrison

Acknowledgments

Thank you to my editor, Lisa Barnett, and to all the people at Heinemann; to professor and playwright, Gary Garrison; to my playwriting teachers, Mrs. Mary Bill, Young Playwright's Inc., and Linda Eisenstein; to my students and the faculty and administration at Lake Ridge Academy; and those of you who could see possibilities in what seemed impossible.

Introduction

I took a break from writing this book and went to have my hair done. Gloria is my hairdresser. After sitting all day in front of a computer, she is the dispenser of a special kind of nirvana. Gloria asked what I was doing this summer and I said that I was writing a book about playwriting. She continued to slather my hair with something that smelled like heaven, asking polite questions about the book. But, when I told her the title of the book, she became animated and energized. "I saw a sandal on the road yesterday. How did that shoe get there? Was some kid sticking his foot out the window? God forbid that an accident took place there and a shoe was left behind. When I see a kid's shoe, I get the chills" . . . and on and on.

It happens to me all the time. When I mention shoes on the highway, the reaction is instantaneous recognition and enthusiastic conjecturing. "How did that shoe get there? And why is there only one shoe?" I've talked to some people who have actually seen how a shoe ended up on the highway. But there are more unexplained shoes out there. And they make people think and wonder.

The reason I first started taking pictures of these shoes was purely artistic. The image of one shoe alone on the side of the road was a haunting image that made a great picture. It was also a metaphor to me. It said something about our society. Cars rush past these shoes, their drivers absorbed in morning coffee, cell phone conversations, and mental lists of things to do. They don't have time to stop and wonder about a shoe. I thought of all the people alone in the world who are like that shoe, living on the very edge of society. So I began to photograph the shoes.

And there were *lots* of them. I was astonished to realize that there were also all *kinds* of shoes on the road. I found a dress shoe, a work boot, a Winnie the Pooh sneaker, a pair of sandals, clogs, even a Doc Martin. And I found them at the oddest times. Easter morning I saw a navy blue ladies dress shoe in the road outside a church. Was someone in a hurry to get to sunrise services? Did they suddenly look down at their feet in the middle of a "Hallelujah" and realize that they were wearing only one shoe?

My daughter, who is also a photographer, joined me on these photographic trips. I would drive and she would hop out and shoot. People began to tell us where to find a shoe and we would make a list of places to go to catch the best light of the day and the lightest amount of traffic.

But there was one shoe that made me stop and think. Our family was in a rush to get to a school concert. I saw a tennis shoe on the entrance ramp to the highway we took to get to the school and I asked my husband to stop the car so I could take a picture of it. I jumped out with my camera, which was loaded with film to take pictures of the kids at the concert, and snapped a picture of the tennis shoe. I turned around to get back into the car and saw another shoe; a red dress shoe, covered with grit, lying by a drainage grate. I couldn't believe I hadn't seen it before. I started snapping pictures and one of them became the cover to this book.

I jumped back into the car and the whole family talked about that red shoe. How did it get there? There was no consensus of opinion, but there were a lot of good stories told.

There were good stories behind the shoes. And good stories make good plays. So I began to write my own play about shoes on the highway. And then I shared the pictures with my playwriting students. I asked them what they thought about the shoes. They came up with the most imaginative stories about how the shoes got there, about the characters that put the shoes on the road, and on and on. The pictures made them think and wonder. The pictures really helped them write monologues and scenes and plays.

The shoes were the beginning. This book is the result of six years of teaching playwriting to youngsters by using visual and audio cues. These chapters have been used not only in my classroom, but in classrooms across the United States. They've been used by language arts teachers who want to teach a unit on playwriting and by theatre teachers who are looking for ideas to energize their playwriting students.

This book is not a "how to" book on writing plays. There are plenty of books out there already. This book is the answer to the questions writing teachers hear a least a hundred times a year. Questions like, "What am I supposed to write about?" or "I can't think of anything to write. Where do I start?" This book is also for teachers who want to try something different, to risk, to bring characters and stories to life onstage, and to write a play. I believe that there is no other form of writing that is so exciting to teach.

I hope that you will enjoy this book and use the ideas in your classroom. I hope that if something doesn't work you will adapt it to fit your students and their particular needs. I hope that this book becomes one of those books with random pieces of paper stuck in the chapters you like the most. I hope that it refuses to stay shut on your desk because the corners are folded over from so much use. And I hope that you will write to me *MaureenBJohnson@aol.com* and let me know what works and what you've changed to fit your course. And most of all, let me know if you see any shoes out there.

Chapter Summaries

Take a Quick Look

Chapter 1 The significant object monologue and its subsequent variations are a vital part of my playwriting course. The advice of my playwriting teachers, to start simple, was solid and has proven very effective.

Chapter 2 Every playwright has felt the characters come alive on a page of dialogue. I really believe that when you allow your young playwrights to wear the character, they start to understand on a very visceral level how important strong, well-defined characters are to their writing.

Chapter 3 My students continued to write random, overheard phrases in their journals for the rest of the semester. These phrases were used as titles and themes for plays, opening lines for characters, and as inspiration for class scene work.

Chapter 4 My students are passionate about their music. They talk about it, analyze it, move to it, and watch video interpretations of it. Music is as much of an inspiration to them as it was to my generation. How could I channel this passion and use it as an inspiration for playwriting? After all, plays bend time and place just like music.

Chapter 5 Shaking up a young playwright by asking him to write about juxtaposing images in a photograph or to create a set of pieces from random, unrelated objects can lead to the "Ah ha" moment we all yearn for when we see a play. As the playwrights look at the juxtaposition of images, they experience the "Ah ha" of discovering relationships. With this visceral experience, it is much easier for them to create such a moment for their audiences as they write.

Chapter 6 Using the rock pictures has led to some very interesting dialogues. There have been many different interpretations of the same rock picture and message. . . . Some rock dialogues have grown into short plays when playwrights have added more scenes leading up to the painting of a rock. All of the students like the idea that the act of painting a rock gives energy and movement to their scenes.

Chapter 7 I used shoes as a visual cue because they provoked me to think. Why was there only one shoe? How did the shoe get on the side of the road? What does a lonely shoe say about our society where everything is disposable? Is the shoe a metaphor for something else? Growing old? Being alone? . . . I've learned that there's a story for every shoe on the highway. And "story" and "character" are what playwriting is all about.

Shoes on the Highway

1 Significant Object Monologue

The teaching year usually begins with a class of very tentative students. They love plays. They've seen them. They know what they like and dislike about them. Now they want to try their hand at writing them. And they don't know where to begin. And they're a bit overwhelmed with a form of writing that they've never tried before. Where to begin? It's my job to help them.

Beginnings are significant. Especially when you are a teacher and you want to set the tone for the semester or perhaps the year. I wanted them to write, not run in fear of playwriting to the administration with course transfer sheets. So, when I was designing my course, I went back to my own playwriting teachers for advice.

My playwriting teachers told me, "Keep it simple." It applied in so many ways. Story, character, conflict, dialogue—and on and on—until every aspect of playwriting was covered by "keeping it simple." So when I was writing the curriculum for my playwriting class, this theme reverberated in my head.

Simple implied clarity. Simple implied easy to follow. In theatre it doesn't get much simpler than a monologue.

I liked the idea of beginning with something simple and then building on it. One character speaking alone onstage. Lit by one light from above. Very dramatic. Very simple. One character speaking with passion about . . . what? It was my job to help them figure that out.

At the same time *I* was trying to figure this out, I saw the movie *Children of Heaven.* It is a story about two children that share a pair of shoes. But, it is much more than that. The film takes the simplest of objects, a pair of shoes, and makes some powerful statements about courage, endurance, and love. I began to think of all the plays and movies I'd seen in which a simple, significant object, which holds great meaning to the main character, drives the story.

Then the idea hit me. First, I'd show the class the film, *Children of Heaven.* We'd discuss the film, the shoes, the conflicts, and the story. This would then lead to a discussion of simple, significant objects that are valued by the main characters of plays that the students had seen or read. Then I'd ask them, *"If your house was burning, what would you grab?"* They would identify some "thing" that they felt passionate about. I would ask them to write a monologue telling the class why this object held such value to them. The significant object monologue was born. I had the idea for the first writing assignment. Now I had to put it into a concrete series of events that made sense.

I realized that everyone in the class might not suddenly share their feelings about an important object in their lives and that I should be the first person to share. If someone went first in explaining the significance of an object it would begin to create an atmosphere of trust. This safe atmosphere is extremely important when it comes to a playwriting class because the students share their work with everyone in the class. When rewriting, a student needs to hear the work read aloud—in front of everyone—which is a mighty scary proposition. It was time to bring out the fake vampire teeth.

The first gift that my husband ever gave me was a set of fake vampire teeth. You know, the plastic, glow-in-the-dark teeth that you put inside your mouth to scare people when you smile. Our first date was a Halloween party. He was dressed as the Monster from the Black Lagoon and I was dressed as Raggedy Ann. He thought it would be a great idea to get me a small gift. As I opened the tissue-wrapped teeth and gazed down at the most unusual present, I realized that this was no ordinary man and if I chose to begin a relationship with him, it would be no ordinary life. So I smiled and said thanks. Raggedy Ann would spend the entire party smiling and wearing vampire teeth.

I had kept the glow-in-the-dark vampire teeth in my jewelry box for thirty years. I knew that it was time to share them with my playwriting class in a significant object monologue. I thought if I went first, maybe the students would begin to trust me and subsequently, each other and we'd be off to a great start.

Writing the Monologues

My students were already familiar with the definition of a monologue. If your students are not, then you may want to pull some examples from plays or even movies and read them in class to familiarize the students with this dramatic form of writing. In the Appendix there is a form (see page 116) that I use for the assignment. It contains some guidelines for the monologue and a space to write the rough draft. (If students create this assignment electronically, remind them to back up their work on their computer *and* a disk. This has saved many students' work when a computer crashes or a hard copy gets lost or misplaced. If the students don't have access to a computer, then just have them use the form as a rough draft and write up another draft to use for their delivery of the monologue in class.)

Reading the Monologues

I told the class that I would like to share my signficiant object with them. I think they were expecting a dried flower or a beautiful ring. As they looked at the glow-in-the-dark vampire teeth, they didn't know if they should laugh or even smile. I began to read my monologue aloud and they began to realize that this was not going to be an ordinary class. After I finished, I asked for more volunteers.

Tom offered to read. He stood up, took off his ratty army jacket that was covered with buttons and patches, and handed it over to the class for examination. He began his monologue. He described the jacket as his memory coat. Every single thing on the jacket had meaning for him. There were pins from a European trip, patches from musicals he had been involved with, and even stains from coffeehouses and fast food places he had been with his friends.

As he spoke, the coat took on new meaning. It was his protection, his collection of memories, his story. When he finished reading, the class applauded. Of course, no one wanted to go next. But we traveled through each and every monologue. Some were better than others. One student wrote about his computer, another about his car. Another student wrote about a photo album, another about a diary she had been keeping since the second grade. All of the monologues shared a bit of the person with the class. It was a good beginning.

The next step was to throw in some conflict. After we had finished reading all of the monologues aloud (and that can take up two or three class periods), I told them the next writing assignment would build on this monologue. They would write a new monologue in which the object they valued so deeply was taken away, stolen, lost, or destroyed. An imaginary situation had to be created and they were allowed to introduce another character who would only be spoken *to* by the main character. It was still a monologue.

The conflict was an important element to this assignment. As writers, they had to make the conflict simple and clear to their audience. By the end of this monologue, the conflict had to be resolved. The resolution did not have to be happy. I told the class that this exercise would be graded. It had to be one page in length and they were to follow the guidelines that we had established for the first monologue.

The next three classes were devoted to reading the new monologues aloud. This process of reading aloud from the very beginning of class sets the stage, so to speak, for the longer readings of scenes and plays later in the semester. It also creates a mind-set for the students. Everything they write in this class must be heard. Beginning with a short, simple assignment read aloud, they begin to train their minds to listen for what will work onstage and what will not; what sounds natural and what does not. Reading aloud also catches overlooked grammatical errors.

Tom read his monologue first. He wrote of a time in the future when he moved to a new school. At his new school, he was not allowed to wear his jacket. He had to wear a uniform because there was a strict dress code. He spoke to the dean of discipline in his monologue, trying to explain how important it was for him to wear his coat. The conflict was resolved with Tom running away from the school and returning to his old school.

The following monologue was written by Russ. The conflict is introduced almost immediately: His favorite statue of a wolf is found cracked and broken. It is a first draft and uses the metaphor of the wolf figurine and its broken state compared to the entire species of wolves and their strength and pride.

Cracked Paws
by Russ

I remember the day I walked in on it. Broken. Its paws were cracked. The wolf sculpture I worked so hard to buy when I was a kid, broken. I ran all around the house looking for the super glue so I could put it back together. Make the wolf whole again.

I didn't know why I felt so strongly about the wolf sculpture. Maybe it's because I worked so hard to earn the money to buy it. Maybe it was because the money used to buy it went to help the wolves. Or maybe it was because of the beauty of the species.

A wolf's pride is much like that of humans. It's protected with every ounce of energy and this energy gives it the will to live, run, play, hunt and survive. When the wolf cries everyone hears. The pain and sorrows of life fill the night.

Like so many other things in this world, wolves are misunderstood . . . viewed as something they are not. But all of the misunderstanding in the world will never break the beauty and pride of the species.

The other monologues had conflicts ranging from siblings who destroyed the objects, mothers who threw the objects away, to someone who searched frantically throughout the monologue to find the object they had misplaced. The class realized that by adding a conflict, the stakes were raised and the monologues became much more interesting. They also agreed that watching someone onstage searching frantically for an object was much more interesting than listening to someone speak standing perfectly still. We took time to discuss these elements.

Now they were ready for their next and final monologue. The students would stretch their dramatic writing ability a little bit more. This assignment built on the first two assignments but relied almost completely on their imaginations and their ability to convey attachment, conflict, and resolution.

For this assignment, you assemble a collection of unusual objects. These objects can be pieces of clothing, random things we use in our everyday life, or even antiquities. There should be twice the number of objects as there are students in your class. Over the years, I've collected:

- fake leopard fur hats
- an old diary
- pieces of costume jewelry
- old dolls
- old books
- family pictures
- a coffee mug
- purses and ladies gloves
- pipes
- old shoes
- silk flowers
- seashells
- garden gloves
- old tools
- an old autograph book
- old magazines
- records, tapes, CDs, and their matching cases
- a couple of wooden boxes with random objects inside

The objects are spread out on a table before the students enter the room. Once they are settled, I ask them to walk around the table covered with objects. I ask them not to touch the objects but simply to look at them and decide on one object they find intriguing.

I pick up an object and begin to speak about it. I tell a story of its importance to me. This five-minute story should be as convincing as possible. It should have the students believing that what I say is absolutely true. This story should include a conflict and a resolution involving the object.

After the end of the story, I ask the class, "How many of you believe that this story is true?" A majority of hands should go up. I tell them that it is all imaginary and give them the requirements of the final monologue.

This assignment involves choosing an object from the table, investing it with importance and emotional connections, adding a conflict, and resolving this conflict. All of it must be totally fabricated and imaginary. Even the character that speaks in the monologue must be imaginary.

The actual choosing of objects can take place in the following ways.

- You can go oldest to youngest or vice versa and allow the students to go to the table to pick up their object.
- You can line everyone up according to their birthdays. Begin with January.
- You can leave the objects on the table and allow the students to go one at a time to examine the object they choose. The objects stay on the table. This way, the students choose some of the same objects and they come up with some very different approaches to the same object.
- I never let the objects go home with the students. They are notoriously absentminded and I've lost a lot of objects.

Variations

A variation on this exercise is to take a field trip to a local Goodwill or Salvation Army thrift store. The amount of money to be spent on the object is agreed upon in advance. Set a size limit as well because someone will undoubtedly want to bring home a giant Mediterranean-style floor lamp or incredibly ornate end table. Let the students roam around until they find an intriguing object. After about an hour's time, everyone checks out with their object and your entire class has contributed to a good cause, namely, the charity that runs the store! The idea of a treasure hunt to find just the right object also increases the students' investment in the writing assignment.

If your school doesn't have the money to spend on such an assignment, the following approach works just as well. Ask each student to bring in an everyday household object. They deposit their objects on the table and then pick up an object someone else brought into class. This approach challenges the students to imagine how such an everyday object could possibly be of such passionate importance to a character.

The following pieces are first drafts of the significant object monologue. Some are the very first monologues written by the students using something from their lives that they treasure while others add conflict and imaginary situations to the original assignment.

In the first piece, Tom has a juggling book that he considers very important. Even at this early stage in the playwriting course, Tom uses metaphor in his monologue. He gives subtle hints that he is not only learning to juggle but that his stressful life is a juggling act, too.

Natural Laws of Life

by Tom

(Reading from book)

"First of all, practice in front of a wall so that you *can't* throw them too far in front of you."

(Tries to juggle bean bags, but fails, frustrated scream)

I'll never get this! Why do books always make it seem so simple to do things? Who was the brain behind this book anyway? Well, I'm sure they didn't have the juggling book from hell to teach them. They probably work for the circus and get paid to juggle. Cheaters.

(Tries juggling again, does better, but still drops them)

Oh, I give up! What's the use anyway? My parents were right. I'm never gonna be able to juggle and it was a waste of money and time. Twelve freakin' dollars. I could've made these things for cheaper.

(Sits and thinks, mimics parents)

"You'll never be able to ride a bike. You'll never learn to ski. You'll never learn this multiplication table."

(Pause, thinks, looks up)

But I did . . . all of those . . . P-ph! No! My parents were wrong. I can do whatever I wanna do! I'm nine years old! I'm an adult! At least at buffet restaurants and amusement parks anyway. I'm gonna juggle. I'll show them what I can do.

(Juggles, messes up, but keeps trying about three times until finally gets it)

I got it! I got it!

(Drops bean bags)

Well, it's better than any of my other attempts. Oh, I wonder what my parents are gonna say when they see me juggling! They're going to be so proud of me! I can't wait to show them! But I've gotta practice more before showing off. Now let's see here.

(Reading from book)

"For a beginning juggler, the produce department of any grocery store can take on a wonderful new dimension." Hm . . .

(Big smile)

This next piece was written by Aaron after adding a conflict to the original monologue. It alludes to a relationship and the significance of the ring and its loss. The resolution is also a clever bit of business.

The Ring

by Aaron

Where the heck is my ring?! Dangit! I haven't misplaced that thing since I got it! Jamie will flip if I tell her I lost all of my jewelry including the necklace she bought me for Christmas.

Alright, Aaron, think. Where did you take it off? Umm . . . I know I took it off before I went dirt-biking at Michaela's, but did I leave it at my house, Jamie's, or Michaela's? I haven't seen it anyplace that I'd normally leave my rings. I'll have to ask Michaela if she's seen any unfamiliar jewelry at her house. I just need to make sure Jamie doesn't overhear me talking to anyone about it.

(Pause)

I can't believe we were wearing the same ring. It was so amazing when we both looked down at each other's hand at the same time at camp. We thought that maybe it was a sign of some sort when I bought the same ring five minutes after she did, not knowing if she had even bought anything from the store.

(Pause)

And who would have know we'd be together in a month. But now it's been ten months! It's been so long and I held onto the ring. I can't lose it *now!* I can't believe this . . .

All right . . . Room . . . check. Bookbag . . . check. Dresser . . . check. Desk . . . check. Dirty cloths . . . check. Top of nightstand . . . check. Drawer of nightstand . . . Let's see . . . knife, pens, markers, flashlight, deodorant, *extra contacts that I need to put in to see,* rings, batteries, thumbtacks . . . Oh, wait! My rings!

This next piece is by one of my most imaginative students, Nick. He chose a brick as his favorite object. Highly unusual, but it works! Obviously, this piece takes the monologue assignment into the realm of the imaginary.

The Brick

by Nick

The window hit the brick. Or did the brick hit the window? The window was bigger, but the brick was moving. However the brick was inanimate, so did I hit the window? Perhaps the window hit me. Regardless the brick won, or I won. Well, either way, the window lost.

> Running seemed like the thing to do. I guess the cops felt the same. In retrospect it may not have been the best decision. Cops hate it when you run. I would too, if I were them. Down an alleyway, over a fence I go. Across a busy street. Well, not entirely across. I smash into a Ford Taurus at full sprint.
>
> I know I hit the Taurus and the Taurus hit me. The alternative is too hard to consider. I was nearly run over by a Mack Truck soon thereafter. Despite this I got up, just to be impacted by a police car. My legs were snapped, streaming pain down my spine to my head. I tired to crawl under the badly dented car, but a strong hand grabbed me by one of my mangled limbs and pulled me out. Although I didn't feel the boot against the back of my head, I felt my face slam hard against the cold, menacing concrete.
>
> And I was done. There was no more fight left in me and I could run no more.

Some other variations for this assignment can be intriguing to explore. The students can write the monologue from a different point of view. For example, take the case of Tom's jacket and the administrator who must uphold the dress code. The student could write a monologue for the administrator. Perhaps the administrator's job is on the line. Perhaps he has let the dress code lapse in several previous incidents and has been told to get tough with the students or he'll lose his job. Perhaps this same administrator was a war protestor in the '60s and believes that Tom has a right to wear his jacket.

The two monologues can then be delivered side by side. The playwright could intertwine the monologues; first Tom speaks for a paragraph and then the administrator speaks. Then we return to Tom's monologue and so on, until the two monologues are finished. This variation can lead to an exploration of dialogues and their effectiveness in a play.

The following piece was performed as part of our evening of original plays. It is a variation that presents the first character's monologue, then another character's reaction to that monologue, and finally, a return to the first character and another reaction. This is an excerpted version called "Partners in Chipmunk" by Michael. (We actually had a chipmunk head for the performers to use.)

> *The apprentice chipmunk*
>
> You know those big furry animals you see walking around amusement parks? Yeah. That's me. Yes, I am a character . . . literally. I

was hoping for a job in one of those snazzy song and dance shows. You know what I'm talking about, right? I just love the excitement backstage, the sound of applause, giving entertainment to the people . . . but instead, I am getting paid to walk around in a costume. A chipmunk costume. Do you know how hot it gets in that thing? Once I thought I was going to pass out from the heat. I needed a drink. So I took one. Out of the hand of an old lady. It didn't make my partner too happy. He's got a lot of seniority. He's a twenty-year veteran character. He's always talking about the good old days of 1981 . . . the best years of his life. Yada yada yada. He does a quality job but I never stop hearing the complaints about my performance. He tries to help me. He makes me stand in front of a mirror in the changing room and says, "Make your character smile." How do you make a big hunk of plastic sitting on top of your head smile? This is not the high point of my acting career.

The veteran chipmunk
I've had many partners in my years as part of the chipmunk team but the latest one is the least enthusiastic of all. Being a character performer is an honorable job. I can still remember my first day in 1981. The warm weather, the happiness of the people surrounding me . . . what a great job! It is my calling in life to bring joy to all the little children who come my way. I can't understand the dismal attitude of my partner . . . I've been trying to give him some tips . . . to become ONE with chipmunk. He doesn't understand . . . I think I'll be able to whip him into shape eventually. Then he might realize how lucky he is.

The apprentice chipmunk
Yeah. Real lucky. The other day my partner wanted me to energize, in costume. It isn't already hot enough in that costume but now I have to run around sweating in it just to energize . . . to be ONE with the character . . . The result of all this is a dirty sock type of smell that seems to seep into my pours and remains with me for the rest of the day. I had a lunch date with Snow White and all during lunch she kept making weird faces and sniffing. That's what my date consisted of . . . Snow White scrunching up her nose as if to say, Did you cut the cheese? I've tried to get rid of the smell but I just can't. It's part of me now. Maybe that's what my partner means by becoming *ONE* with the character.

Another variation is to read the two monologues side by side and then have the characters turn toward each other and improvise a dialogue. They must remain true to the characterization and the conflict should continue but now you have the beginnings of a rudimentary dialogue.

Your students might try a monologue that shares with the audience a secret about the object. In the case of the jacket, Tom could share with the audience that the jacket belonged to his dad or grandfather who has passed away. This raises the stakes when the threat of having the jacket confiscated or worse, destroyed, presents itself when the conflict is introduced.

At this point in the course, I have found it to be extremely effective to have the students write a monologue/dialogue/monologue. The same scenario is used; an imaginary, significant object monologue is written. Then a dialogue between the protagonist and the antagonist is written. The final monologue is a return to the protagonist and some sort of resolution of the conflict ends the piece. If your students can hear this three-part piece read by some acting students, it can be invaluable when it comes time for rewriting.

A Word About Rewrites: A Fact of Playwriting Life

I can't tell you how many times I've spent the good part of the first two months of a playwriting course building the students' confidence in writing plays only to have them come to me with a first draft of a scene and say, "I can't think of anything to rewrite." Or, "I don't know where to go with this. I think this scene is finished." I usually tell them the story of plays that I started years ago that are still being rewritten. There is a teacher on staff at my school who is a playwright, and I tell her story of a play that has been produced several times and she is still doing rewrites!

The most effective tool in getting this point across is the dramatic staging or read-through of your students' plays. They begin to hear what needs revising in their pieces. Sometimes it is painful to them as they hear stilted dialogue that makes no sense at all. But it is a lesson worth the pain. They go back to the script and get to work. They begin to ask for more dramatic readings so that they can do more rewrites. Seeing and *hearing* is believing when it comes to crafting a better play. A teacher needs to set up a system for these readings by using class members or acting students or, for that matter, faculty members!

Student Work . . . Using Significant Objects as the Source for Writing a Short Play

The following excerpts are from plays that were written by my playwriting students. The first play was written using a pumpkin as the significant object. Jonathan went on with this piece to become one of eight finalists in a national playwriting contest sponsored by Young Playwrights, Inc. He spent nine days in New York City working on his play and hearing the works of the other young playwrights. It was a life-changing experience.

Young Playwrights, Inc. is a fantastic resource for young playwrights. The critiques that they send to the students about their plays are worth their weight in gold! Check out their website at *www.writeaplay.com* for information about their contests and workshops.

Conversation with a Pumpkin

by Jonathan

Characters

RICHARD, 16 A sleep-deprived loner; an acquaintance of Silverman
PUMPKIN, NA A talking carved pumpkin, placed on the front step
SILVERMAN, 17 A popular jock, sponsor of the house party. Rachel's older brother
RACHEL SILVERMAN, 16 Silverman's younger sister (She is dressed completely in black. Currently in charge of dealing with the trick-or-treaters who come to the front door.)
TRICK-OR-TREATERS (five to eight) A large group of costumed neighborhood children, including an Angel (the group spokesperson), a Devil, a Ghost, a Prophet, and a Princess Leia
GIRLS #1 & 2, 17 Two visitors to Silverman's party

Setting: The front stoop of the Silverman household, currently the site of an uproarious house party.

Time: Halloween Night, 2001. Just after midnight.

At Rise: *The front stoop of a large house. A large* CARVED PUMPKIN *sits on the front step. Also on the front step is* RICHARD*—a teenager, curled into a ball and with his hat jammed down around his eyes.*

*Inside of the house—sounds of a loud, large party. The door opens—*SILVERMAN, *another teenager, peers out at* RICHARD's *immobile body. The sounds of the party leak out with him.*

SILVERMAN: Hey, Richard. Rich. (*Beat; louder*) RICHARD! Hey, you awake there?

RICHARD: Eat s**t and die.

SILVERMAN: What'd you say?

RICHARD: Shut the door. I'm trying to sleep.

SILVERMAN: Out here?

RICHARD: Yes.

SILVERMAN: Why?

RICHARD: *(Growls under breath)*

SILVERMAN: Don't you think you should come inside, dude? It's cold out there.

RICHARD: Too loud.

SILVERMAN: What?

RICHARD: It's too damn loud in there. Go away.

SILVERMAN: Okay, man. Whatever.

He shuts the door and goes back inside. RICHARD *shoots a glare at his back and then settles down again. A pause.*

PUMPKIN: Do you have the time?

At this point, the PUMPKIN *begins to speak to* RICHARD. *There is some dialogue between the two and then* RICHARD *notices that he is talking to a pumpkin. It says a lot about his current state of mind that he checks his watch.*

RICHARD: Twelve-oh-five.

PUMPKIN: Happy November.

RICHARD: What's so happy about November?

PUMPKIN: Watch your back.

RICHARD: What?

Door opens and hits RICHARD *in the back.* TWO GIRLS*—the openers of the door—immediately start to giggle. The girls cross offstage and the conversation continues.*

PUMPKIN: Why are you tired?

RICHARD: Was up all last night. Got maybe three hours of sleep.

PUMPKIN: What for?

RICHARD: Essay. Plus a Chem test.

PUMPKIN: Did it matter?

RICHARD: Nah. Both sucked. Entire day sucked, actually. Then I went home and had a fight with my parents, just to finish things off in style.

PUMPKIN: How fascinating. Watch it.

RACHEL SILVERMAN *enters. She is a year older than Richard, and dresses all in black. She sees Richard, who plays dead. She carefully steps over him and enters the house.*

RICHARD: That was nice of her.

PUMPKIN: At least she didn't step on you.

RICHARD: Yeah. Fills me with a warm glow.

The conversation continues until the Trick-or-Treaters enter.

PUMPKIN: Here we go.

Enter a large group of TRICK-OR-TREATERS, *none older than nine—including a* DEVIL, *an* ANGEL, *a* GHOST, *a* PROPHET, *and perhaps a* PRINCESS LEIA. *Richard plays dead.*

TRICK-OR-TREATERS: *(In unison)* Trick or treat! *(Beat)* TRICK OR TREAT!

The ANGEL *goes up to* RICHARD *and pokes him.* RICHARD *opens one eye.*

ANGEL: Hey, mister. Got any candy?

RICHARD: No. No candy here.

ANGEL: But your porch light is on.

RICHARD: 'snot my porch light.

ANGEL: Then why are you sitting here?

RICHARD: It's my friend's house. Go away.

ANGEL *steps over* RICHARD, *and knocks on the door.*

ANGEL: TRICK OR TREAT!

TRICK-OR-TREATERS: *(Join in on "or")* OR TREAT!

RICHARD *jumps to his feet—knocking aside the* ANGEL*—and runs at the group screaming at the top of his lungs. The kids,* *terrified, run off the stage. Richard chases, then returns to the front step and sits down.*

PUMPKIN: Well-handled.
RICHARD: Shut up.

The door opens. RACHEL *appears, holding a basket of candy.*

RACHEL: Hey—were there some kids just here?
RICHARD: *No.*

Lays back down on the stoop.

RACHEL: Look, are you trying to sleep out here or something?
RICHARD: Good one, Sherlock.
RACHEL: You could use the study, you know. There's a couch in there. I'm not using it right now. (*Beat*)
RICHARD: Really?
RACHEL: Third door from the left upstairs.

Richard hesitates

Last time I checked, there's central heating. You might want to look into it.

RICHARD: (*Beat*) No thanks. I'm okay.
RACHEL: Out here?
RICHARD: I've got a jacket. I'm all right.
RACHEL: You're sure?
RICHARD: Yeah. Thanks.
RACHEL: (*Studies Richard for a second*) Okay. If you're sure.

RACHEL *shuts the door.* RICHARD *lies back down on the stoop. Beat.*

RICHARD: (*Softly*) Shit.
PUMPKIN: Why didn't you take her up on that?
RICHARD: I don't know.
PUMPKIN: You don't know?
RICHARD: *I don't know.*
PUMPKIN: (*Beat*) Want to know your future?
RICHARD: Not really.
PUMPKIN: You're going to die. Very soon. Give it maybe two or three hours.
RICHARD: Sounds good.
PUMPKIN: Really. You're going to die.

(*Beat; calculating tone*)
But before that, you're going to fall in love.
(*Beat*)

RICHARD: *I'm* going to fall in love?

PUMPKIN: That's right.

RICHARD: (*Beat*) Whatever.

PUMPKIN: Really. Romeo and Juliet style.

RICHARD: You're full of b*****it.

PUMPKIN: You'll fall in love, and then you'll die. Three hours.

RICHARD: First, I'm not going to die. Second, I'm not going to fall in love.

PUMPKIN: You don't think you're going to fall in love?

RICHARD: Yes.

PUMPKIN: Yes, you are going to fall in love?

RICHARD: No, I'm not going to fall in love.

PUMPKIN: Not ever?

RICHARD: Not in the next three hours.

PUMPKIN: Why not?

RICHARD: Because, honestly, I don't like people. I don't like being around them for too long.

PUMPKIN: If you don't like people, why are you out here?

RICHARD: To try and get away from them!

PUMPKIN: Which doesn't change the fact that you're going to fall in love, and then you're going to die.

RICHARD: Did you hear a single word I just said?

PUMPKIN: (*Continuing*) In three hours. Love before death. Death after love.

RICHARD: Whatever, okay?

PUMPKIN: Love, death. Death, love.

RICHARD: Okay, now you're starting to get on my nerves.

PUMPKIN: Three hours.

RICHARD: You're annoying me.

PUMPKIN: Love-death-love. Death-love-death.

RICHARD: Okay, that's it. (*Picks up pumpkin and stands up*) Say that one more time and you're airborne, okay? (*A pause*)

PUMPKIN: Three hours. Love, death.

RICHARD: I'll give you three *seconds*!

PUMPKIN: Death, love.

RICHARD: One—

PUMPKIN: Love, death.
RICHARD: Two—
PUMPKIN: Death, love.
RICHARD: Screw you! (*Throws pumpkin*)
PUMPKIN: Love, *death*!

The PUMPKIN *hits the ground and shatters.* RICHARD *freezes, arm still extended. He sits back down on the stoop, perhaps looking a little guilty. The door suddenly opens—*RICHARD *looks up.* RACHEL *looks at him, then at the smashed pumpkin. And then back at him.*

RICHARD: (*Looks down, mumbles*) I need some sleep.

He starts to walk off down the path. RACHEL *watches him go as he exits. Fade to black.*

Using a pumpkin, a talking one at that, takes the significant object piece to an entirely new level of performance. Jonathan has been working on this piece for a few years now. It is part of a larger, full-length work called "The Oberlin Chronicles."

The next excerpt is from the second draft of a play by Kusha. The basketball jersey is its significant object. He begins the play with a monologue by the main character, Larry, and then introduces another character, Jack, described as Larry's antagonistic brother. In the opening monologue, Larry talks about the ritual connected with his jersey before a big game.

The Jersey

by Kusha

Characters
LARRY
JACK

Setting: Larry's bedroom

Time: Before the big basketball game

SCENE 1

At Rise: LARRY *in a spotlight standing at the foot of his bed. As the monologue progresses, the lights come up in the room.*

LARRY: I think about it all day. (*Pause*) The night before the game, I get so excited. The game, and the crowd and the court . . . just the feel of the ball!

(*Pauses to settle down*) I'd go outside the night before and grab the ball and just play, so hard, until I'd fall down exhausted. And I'd want to put it on right then. I'd think, "It's only twenty degrees outside. It's not like it'll get sweaty." And then I'd run in and open my closet and it would be sitting there, the way I had folded and refolded it a hundred times that day. (*Larry picks up the jersey and pauses to look at it*) And then I would put it on. (*Larry puts on the jersey, stands up straight then takes it off and folds it up again*)

The next morning, I'd hear the alarm clock and pause just to think about the game. I'd get up, slowly, get ready for school and right before I'd leave, I would carefully place it in the bag. (*Larry places the jersey in his bag*)

At school, I always put my bag on the top shelf in the commons so no one could put their stuff on top of it. I would think about it all morning and I would check to see if it was still there when I went to get lunch. I would sit in class, shaking my pen, tapping my foot, staring blankly into the depths of the chalkboard thinking about it until finally . . . (*Waits for bell to sound . . . nothing happens*) Finally . . . (*Same thing again*) FINALLY . . . (*The bell sounds and Larry jumps*) Out of class, sprint for my bag, run to the locker room, slowing down at the door. (*Larry puts on his jersey*) I would put it on and look at myself in the mirror.

(Blackout)

SCENE 2

Bedroom. LARRY *is still wearing the jersey.* JACK *enters.*

JACK: What the hell are you doing?

LARRY: (*Quickly taking off the jersey and folding it up*) Nothing. What do you want?

JACK: (*Sitting down on Larry's bed*) Nothing, Lar.

LARRY: Then get the hell out of here. And don't call me that.

JACK: Call you what, Lar? (*Jack picks up the jersey and holds it in front of himself*) I'm the greatest basketball player that ever lived even though I suck at the game.

LARRY: Put it down, Jack.

JACK: (*Wads up jersey and throws it on the floor*) Do you think you're good at basketball, Lar?

LARRY *says nothing, grabs the jersey off the floor, folds it and puts it into his bag.*

JACK: (*Continuing*) Huh, Lar? (*Pause*) You suck.

LARRY: Get out of my room, man. I have a game tomorrow and I want to get some sleep.

JACK: OK, Lar. But you're going to play like shit anyway, so why bother sleeping?

LARRY: (*Glares at him*) What?

JACK *turns as if to exit.* LARRY *turns his back to* JACK. JACK *takes the jersey from the bag and exits.* LARRY *gets into bed. Lights go out.*

This opening scene really sets up the conflict. The audience knows something about the basketball jersey that the main character does not, increasing the tension. The stage is also set for future complications. Why does Jack hate Larry so much? Is he a frustrated athlete? Why does he take the jersey? What happens to the jersey? Can Larry play the game without performing the ritual and the jersey? The basketball jersey monologue is used by the playwright to inspire further scene work and a short play.

The significant object monologue and its subsequent variations are a vital part of my playwriting course. The advice of my playwriting teachers, to start simple, was solid and has proven very effective. This exercise also begins to create an atmosphere of openness and trust among the members of the class. They begin to take risks with their writing and aren't afraid to tackle things like full-length plays with talking pumpkins and stolen basketball jerseys. And when they see, after a few rewrites, an audience reacting to the characters that they have created, it is significant.

2 Wear the Character

When I was in tenth grade, a *long* time ago, I played the part of the ingénue in Moliere's "Learned Ladies." Her name was Henriette and she wore a light and airy flowing costume that was heaven to wear. I felt like the most beautiful girl in the world and practically floated in and out of scenes. As soon as I put on the delightful costume, I became the sweet young French girl with the beautiful name.

When I was in twelfth grade, my drama director did a scene from the play for competition. I played Henriette's older sister, Armande, in this competition. Armande was much more repressed than her sweet, younger sister and the costume was very restricting! It was made of heavy French brocade and corseted with little plastic stays. I could hardly breathe in the costume. But the costume must have helped me in creating the character because I won a gold medal and a scholarship to a summer workshop for my performance.

I thought that I would never be in Moliere's "Learned Ladies" again. After all, I had been in the show two times. But, when I was a junior in college, I played the incredibly uptight mother, Philomente, in a full-length version of the same play. Needless to say, the costume was gorgeous. It was also pulled and laced and as tight as the character I was playing.

The reason I share this story is not to show you how my ability to play more and more irascible, unbending characters as time and my career went on. My reason is to show how a costume can really help a performer get into character. Costumes not only help performers understand a period piece and how a character moves through space wearing corsets and waistcoats of heavy brocade, but the right costume can give the performer the "feel" of a character. If getting into a costume helps a performer create a character, what would it do for a young playwright?

I realized that some of my students had never been in a production. They had never stuffed themselves into a corset or donned a wig. I wondered if wearing a costume, or even part of a costume, would help these playwrights understand a character better. Perhaps as they physically layered themselves with costume pieces and parts, the psychological layering of their characters might come easier.

I began to pull out costumes from our school's costume closets. The collection represented a wide variety of styles and time periods. If you don't have access to your school's costume collection, some colleges or community theatres will lend out costumes for school plays. Perhaps they would lend costumes for the school's playwrights. The playwrights only need the costumes for a few class periods.

If none of these scenarios fit you or your teaching situation, you can purchase some interesting articles of clothing at any thrift or resale store. On certain days of the week or at certain times of the year, thrift stores have bag sales. Customers can pack up a bag full of clothes and buy the entire bag for a dollar or two. I even know a teacher who, year after year, emptied his own closet to costume his plays. So, if worse comes to worse, you can search in your own closet for usable pieces.

After several years of teaching this lesson, my collection held the following pieces:

- strange and wonderful hats
- leather jackets
- a couple of wedding and prom dresses
- some "Victoriana"-type clothing
- old furs
- fantasy or medieval costumes like wizard's capes, kilts, capes
- old, faded housecoats

- 1970s psychedelic print slacks and dresses
- Chinese coats and dresses
- African caftans and dashiki shirts

Before I let the students look at these costumes, they have a series of warm-up discussions and a few writing assignments.

I ask the class to answer the following questions on paper first. A form can be found in the Appendix, page 118 for you to reproduce. Making this a written assignment gives the students time to think on their own and then share their ideas with the rest of the class.

1. When you go home to relax, what clothes do you change into?
2. What are your favorite casual clothes?
3. How do you feel when you wear these clothes?
4. Describe your dressiest outfit.
5. Where and when do you wear these clothes?
6. How do you feel when you wear these clothes?
7. Tell me a story about a time when you got all dressed up *or* tell me a story about a time when you bought a new outfit.

Sharing the Stories

I usually share my story about Easter Sunday at my house when I was growing up. Every year, my sisters and brothers knew that a time would come during January, February, or March when our mother would take us shopping.

This was no ordinary shopping trip. This was to buy Easter clothes. It was a *big* deal. We didn't just purchase dresses or, in the case of my brothers, shirts and pants. Every piece of clothing that we wore, from underwear to undershirts and nice, white ankle socks, was bought to put away in our drawers and closets for Easter morning. And woe to the child who wore any of the Easter clothing before Easter.

Easter morning was full of excitement. We all got up early to find our Easter baskets. After sneaking a fair amount of candy down our throats, we ate a big breakfast together and then got dressed for church. Besides the candy, this was the most exciting part of the day. We dug deep into our closets and dresser drawers and brought forth the clothes we were not allowed to wear until that very day. And when we put on the clothing, we felt new from the inside out.

As I look back at the pictures of our family in our Easter finest, I am struck by the hilarious styles of the day. I distinctly remember a hat that was held on my head with a thin strand of elastic that dug into my chin. There was a bunch of flowers at a rakishly dangerous angle on the side of the hat that honestly looked like a dinner plate turned upside down. But as I look at the smile on my face, I can see how proud I was to wear that hat. I felt like the luckiest kid who had ever lived to wear a hat that resembled an upside-down dinner plate. I felt good in those clothes.

After I embarrass myself a bit by telling my clothes story, the students seem more willing to share theirs. A teacher can contribute a lot to the atmosphere of openness and sharing in a classroom by getting the sharing starting. The creation of this kind of atmosphere in a playwriting class, where reading aloud is vital to the success of your young writers, is very important.

When the students share their stories, I ask them questions that start them thinking about possible conflicts that might arise around the type of clothing that they chose to wear. I tell them the story about the time my brother wore a piece of Easter clothing before it was Easter and what happened to him. They relate stories like "The Prom Dress That Got Away," bought by someone else before they had a chance to save up the money to buy it. Or stories like "The Day They Broke the Dress Code," or "The Day My Mom Threw Away My Favorite Sneakers." Discussing possible conflicts and situations related to clothing helps set up the next part of the lesson.

There are many ways to present the costumes to the class. Sometimes I just lay them on tables. Other times I have them hanging on two or three freestanding clothes trees. If you have the use of a theatre space, you can lay them out on the edge of the stage. However you decide to do it, there must be room to spread them out for the students to get a good look at them.

You also have to decide how you are going to have the students pick out their costumes. I always try to have twice as many costumes as the number of students so that everyone is able to pick one thing that they can really relate to. You may want to let students choose by order of age or by random selection. By the end of class, every student should have a costume piece to prompt a character idea.

One year I had a class of six girls. Each one of them chose distinctly different outfits. Their choices were:

- a wedding dress
- a wizard's cape
- a black-and-white 1940s era dress
- an old, faded housedress from the 1950s
- a psychedelic print dress from the 1970s
- a Victorian black-and-white high-collared dress

East student wore the outfit during the first class and talked about how it made her feel. The students then wrote these reflections in their journals. We brainstormed as a class for the type of characters they could create; the wants and needs for these characters and the potential conflicts that they could imagine. These ideas were added to their journals. Some of their suggestions were:

- a bride who was left at the altar
- a wizard whose magic had failed
- a woman at a funeral in a black dress
- a neglected ninety-year-old in an old housedress
- a faded Las Vegas lounge singer
- a jilted Victorian woman whose entire existence depended on marrying the "right" man

The advantage to taking all this time in discussion and brainstorming is that it helps the students with layering a character. Writing it all down keeps the ideas fresh and unforgotten. It also encourages students to add important details or bits of dramatic business to their characters.

For example, one student added a walker as a prop to her character. She spent some time walking around the room with the walker while wearing the faded housecoat. It was an extremely visceral experience and the idea of adding the walker was the idea given to her by another student in the class.

Another student added a pair of oversized glasses to her 1970s psychedelic outfit. Immediately the character developed vision problems—failing to recognize fans asking for autographs. This introduced conflict as the character became belligerent toward her dwindling fan base. Another suggestion was to have the aging star smoke cigarettes. This idea was added and then later discarded. A hacking cough that was a result of the smoking was kept and it definitely helped the student's character creation.

All of these additions came from suggestions made during the brainstorming sessions. This preliminary work with discussion and suggestions made by the class is really worth the time it takes. I've found that most students need help developing characters through layering. I've been given character questionnaires to fill out in many of the writing classes I've taken. These questionnaires are helpful and ask such questions as, "What food does your character like?" or "What is the biggest problem that faces your character?" But I have found that a visceral experience like "wearing" the character really appeals to a host of other senses that might be overlooked in compiling a list of character traits on paper.

Another way to get your students talking about a character is to pass around one or two pieces of clothing. Let the class members feel it or try it on. Then, as a class, make a list of the possible characteristics of a person who would buy and wear such an article of clothing. Give the character potential names, occupations, beliefs, and quirks. Then pass around another piece of clothing and repeat the process.

When you fill the board with traits, ask the students which pieces of clothing they want to use to create their character and character monologues. The students should copy down in their journals the pertinent information about their character. Then as an assignment, they should write up a monologue for that character.

These monologues are most effective when the playwrights are wearing the costumes. If you are fortunate enough to have acting students help out with a dramatic reading, then they should wear the costume. The requirements for these monologues should be the same as the earlier writing assignment. You might want to add another dimension to this monologue by having the character mention the article of clothing in the monologue, but that is up to you.

"Wearing the Character" Play

The following play was written by Ryan. He used a couple of pairs of doctor's scrubs as inspiration for his piece. This short play illustrates how a monologue can grow if a student chooses to extend it and do a number of rewrites. Many of the shorter pieces that the students wrote were later rewritten and lengthened. This particular piece was part of our lunchtime series of dramatic readings.

The "F" Word

by Ryan

Characters

FRANK EMS worker. He's more experienced. He has been on the job so long little fazes him
JIMMY New on the job. He is unsure how to respond to what's going on
LAURA The typical high school girl
DAVID An innocent and nice guy. He's naïve, though, which makes him the victim

Setting: High school

At Rise: DAVID *and* LAURA *are sitting on a bench talking. They are holding hands and cuddling, indicating that they are an item.* FRANK *and* JIMMY *are offstage. They are dressed as* EMTs, *with all the appropriate gear.*

DAVID: So how was the Chem test?

LAURA: Oh, it went fine. (*She grins and snuggles up to him*)

DAVID: (*Pause. Awkwardly*) Um, do you want to know how my test went?

LAURA: (*Eyes closed, still snuggling, looking content*) No.

DAVID: (*Pause*) So, what do you think about going to see a movie this weekend?

LAURA: I don't know . . .

DAVID: But I already cancelled a road trip with my buddies because I thought you'd want me to spend time with you this weekend. You're always saying that we don't get a chance to be alone so, here's the chance.

LAURA: I know, but recently, I've been thinking.

DAVID: (*Pause*) About what?

LAURA: Well, it's us. I just don't think we're working out as a couple.

DAVID: (*Shocked*) But, why! We have tons of stuff in common . . . I do pretty much everything you ask me to do. I'm a complete gentleman . . .

LAURA: I know. I know. I just can't explain why I can't be with you.

DAVID: So, you're breaking up with me?

LAURA: Yes, but don't think of it that way.

DAVID: (*Eyes going wide*) Why . . . what way should I think of it?

LAURA: Just because we aren't dating doesn't mean we can't still hang out.

DAVID: (*Getting up quickly. He knows what's coming*) Oh no, please no! Mercy! *For the love of all . . . don't . . . !*

LAURA: (*Ignoring him, and keeping her "easy-let-down" tone*) *Let's just be friends.*

DAVID: Ahhhh!!!!!

DAVID *falls to the ground as though he has been shot. The actor then begins to pantomime some type of mortal injury, rolling on the ground, gasping in agony.*

LAURA: See, it won't be that bad. Now we're free to see other people. (*Smiles*) I'm glad you're cool with it. See you later, buddy!

When LAURA *says "buddy,"* DAVID'S *convulsions increase in fervor.* LAURA *exits off left. Just as she leaves,* FRANK *and* JIMMY *rush on to where* DAVID *is still on the floor convulsing.*

FRANK: Holy crap, this looks bad.

JIMMY: What is it, what do we got? Heart attack? Asthma? Ebola?

FRANK: Shh! (*Frank shines a light into David's eyes and goes through other typical examination procedures.*) Look at me son. How many fingers am I holding up?

DAVID: (*With difficulty*) A bunch . . .

FRANK: Okay now, son, what's your name?

DAVID: David.

FRANK: David. All right David, you're gonna be okay. Tell me what happened. (*Frank looks down at David who goes into slightly less violent shakes. David looks up at Frank and speaks unsteadily*)

DAVID: She said . . . just . . . fr . . . fr . . . (*Frank covers David's mouth*)

JIMMY: What? Heat stroke? Dysentery?

FRANK: No. (*Attaching an EKG*) Worse. It's the double "O" one.

JIMMY: (*Confused*) What's that?

FRANK: Double "O" one. The single most horrible thing to happen to a man. It's a *"Just_Riends"* (*Frank is careful not to fully say the phrase; however David jumps and begins convulsing when he hears the words spoken. EKG goes crazy)* Calm down, son. (*Trying to hold David down. He calms)* It's OK, I didn't actually say it.

JIMMY: What? That's all? Someone said "just friends"? (*David convulses, EKG beeps)*

FRANK: (*Angry at Jimmy)* What are you trying to do, kill him!?

JIMMY: This is crazy, I just said "just friends." (*David shakes, EKG sounds)* Sorry. How can those two words be so terrible?

FRANK: (*Pulling a blanket out of his box of equipment, he helps David back to the bench, wrapping him in the blanket)* Those "two words" just happen to be the foulest linguistic alliance in all of the history of mankind.

FRANK: With those two words, a woman can bring some poor shmuck like this to his knees.

JIMMY: I think you're overreacting.

FRANK: Well, has anyone ever said it to you?

JIMMY: (*Tries to be confident, but then falters)* No.

FRANK: Exactly. (*Looks at David)* He's stable. C'mon, let's take a walk, I'll explain it. (*They get up and take a walk across stage)* You see, Jimmy, it's one of those things that the majority of guys have to face. The big F. With that phrase alone, just that phrase, a woman you thought was your girl can destroy all that you hold dear. The world that you know can collapse in on itself like a Red Dwarf star being crushed under the awesome weight of its own interstellar mass.

JIMMY: (*Understanding the truth of it)* Wow. I guess I never thought about it really. But, I mean, don't they have reasons for just wanting to be Fr . . . (*Realizing his mistake as EKG gets louder)* Just, ya know?

FRANK: (*Laughs)* Oh, Jimmy. You see, women, they aren't like us men.

JIMMY: Really?

FRANK: Yes. We men, when we do things, have a reason for doing them. Whether we admit it to ourselves, or anyone else, there's meaning behind our actions. With women, that's not the case.

JIMMY: (*Taking a moment to ponder what he's been told)* So, the girl who just did that to poor David, she didn't have a reason for it?

FRANK: Nope. Oh sure, she'll claim there's a good reason. But, if you ask what it is, you'll always get "You won't understand" or "I just don't want to talk about it." It's all a ruse to throw you off the trail. Sometimes they even turn it around and make you feel guilty for asking.

JIMMY: (*They have strolled back to where David is now. They both look at him*) Well, what can we do for him, Frank?

FRANK: Not much we *can* do, Jimmy, just wait it out. He didn't die instantly, that's a good sign. He may just make it. (*Pause*)

JIMMY: Frank?

FRANK: Yeah kid?

JIMMY: Hold me.

They embrace and begin to sing in awesome three-part harmony.

The End

After the performance of the monologues, I require the class to critique each piece. The students can do this with written or oral comments. Sometimes, to save time, I ask for two comments on each piece, one written and one oral. The students then do a rewrite. They hand this final draft in to me for a grade and a critique.

Sometimes I take photos of my students wearing the costumes and delivering the monologues. I then post a good final draft of the monologue along with the pictures on the bulletin board outside my classroom. This further reinforces the idea of wearing a character because other students see the photos, read the monologues, and the characters become very real to them.

Every playwright has felt the characters come alive on a page of dialogue. I really believe that when you allow your young playwrights to wear the character, they start to understand on a very visceral level how important strong, well-defined characters are to their writing.

3 Overheard

I had some incredibly creative teachers in school. I especially remember my eleventh-grade English teacher, Sister Ann. We arrived one day, homework papers in hand, ready to do a lesson on some point of grammar. It was February. It was cold. It was grey. We loved Sister Ann but on this cold, grey day in February, even we would have a hard time staying focused on some weird grammatical bit of information. Thank God, Sister Ann knew that too.

She opened class by saying, "We're going to take a break and study haiku for awhile." I know we should have known what haiku was, but we didn't. She proceeded to read ancient and beautiful examples of haiku. She explained their strict format and their wonderful allusions to the seasons. She played Japanese and Chinese music for us. We were taken away from the greyness and inspired to write and write and write.

After collecting many examples of haiku in our journals, she gave us small pieces of colored paper and asked us to write our best work on the papers. She then had us attach strings of varying lengths to the colored bits of paper and make mobiles by hanging them from hangers. That evening, after we had gone home, Sister Ann hung the hangers from the ceiling of our classroom.

The next day we walked into our classroom and were surrounded by floating haiku. Picture it in your mind: twenty sixteen-year-old girls in a classroom reading haiku as it floated around them on brilliantly colored pieces of paper. These haiku were drawn from the observations surrounding our lives and connected to the beauty of the seasons of the year. I can still feel the poetry as it danced around the room. The strongest lesson I learned that day was that we are surrounded with ideas for writing, for creating poetry, short stories, or plays. We only need to become aware of the possibilities that surround us and take some time to notice them.

Which brings me to the idea for this next exercise: the overheard phrase or conversation. Every day my students hear so many things. They could hardly list all the sounds that surround us. Just like the haiku that hung around the classroom, sounds, phrases, and conversations surround us every day. I've heard and written them in my journal my entire life—hoping to use them at some point; as the title of a play, its theme, or the objective of one of my characters. When students tell me that they can't find anything to write about, I'd tell them to go sit somewhere that was noisy with conversation and write down random phrases that they overheard. Then bring their list of phrases back to class and we'd look for ideas to write about. This suggestion worked on a small scale with individual students and their writer's block. I wondered if it would work with an entire class.

The Difference Between Listening and Hearing

Almost every theatre teacher I've ever had would have us do an exercise that forced us to recognize the difference between hearing and listening. This exercise was simple and effective. The students sit with a paper and pencil in perfect silence. They write down everything that they hear, no matter how insignificant they may think it might be. When about a minute or two has passed, the instructor calls time and leads a discussion by asking the following questions:

- What did you hear?
- What do you think you would hear if we tried this again?
- Do you think you would hear more or less? Why?
- How is listening different than hearing?

Many students will mention noises that no one else has heard. Their awareness of the sounds that surround them every day is really defined. The last question leads to a discussion about how engaged the mind must be in order to listen and not just hear.

At this point, I tell the students a story about going to a flea market. I really like going to flea markets. It's like a treasure hunt to me. Give me something to look for at a flea market and I will try my darndest to find it. But even more exciting than finding treasure is just taking the time to listen to the conversations around me as I walk down the rows and rows of vendors. All kinds of people from all walks of life go to flea markets. All kinds of things are said: comments on the quality of the things for sale; interaction between customers and sellers, customers and their friends. The noise of a flea market can be a rich resource for an astute listener and a creatively "dry" writer.

You can also learn a lot about dialogue as you listen to people speak to each other at a flea market. Conflicting objectives and small dramas are everywhere. Someone wants something and someone else wants to sell it to that person but not at the price they want. A person sees something they have been looking for all day only to lose it to someone who is quicker to pick it up and buy it.

Unique characters are everywhere. I have my favorites: Old Magazine Man who sells the past on pages and whose face is a map of his life; Glass Lady who specializes in Depression glass and whose hair is as blue as the cobalt glassware she sells; Kettle Corn Girl whose smile is refreshingly genuine and who gives free taste tests to all of her smallest customers. Whenever I'm feeling that I don't have an original thought in my head to write about, I go to the flea market and listen.

Listening and Writing Assignment

I ask my students to do the following listening assignment. Go to a place where there will be noisy conversation. Sit for at least ten minutes and write down bits and pieces of what you hear in your journal. The students have to be discrete—no intimate details of classmates and their weekend pursuits, no names, just interesting phrases written down as quickly and as completely as possible. They need a minimum of at least five phrases and preferably fifty phrases if they can write that quickly. They bring these phrases back to class and we will discuss how we can turn them into pieces of theatre.

The next class begins by students sharing the bits and pieces of their overheard conversations. I usually ask them to pick out one or two of their favorites and read them out loud. We list them on the board. The list of phrases may look like this:

- "No drugs in school, Joey"
- "They are going to have to split my jaw apart"
- "Shut up and be nice"
- "Weatherman says a storm's comin' in"
- "She doesn't trust me"
- "You're a dumbass"
- "I'm going to Hell"
- "Nothing more to say"
- ". . . on being Cary Grant"
- "Do you think he knows?"

Then we brainstorm about possible stories that could revolve around the phrases. For example, let's use the one ". . . on being Cary Grant." This phrase could inspire a scene about an office worker who leads a mundane life but in the evening turns into Cary Grant. The Cary Grant persona begins to leak into his daytime personality. He tries to kill off the alter ego when he meets another office worker who reveals that he/she is Grace Kelly. The possible objectives might be for the office worker to keep the "Cary Grant" persona a secret, all the while longing to be Cary Grant.

The following student pieces are scenes that grew out of two different overheard phrases. Students chose where to set the overheard phrase. They could begin with the phrase or they could embed the phrase somewhere in the scene.

"Weather man says a storm's comin' in"
First Draft

Overheard quote dialogue piece by Lakshami

Characters
DORIS
HANK

Setting: An old farmhouse at dinner time with an older married couple

DORIS: Weather man says a storm's comin' in. You git everything done?
HANK: Now, Doris, can't you see I'm tryin' to read up on events?
DORIS: You weren't tryin' anything five seconds ago, Hank.
HANK: Well, I am now, woman. Quiet.
DORIS: Quiet. When the heck have I ever been quiet when something needs sayin'?
HANK: Some things still need doin', I guess.
DORIS: You guess. Well, I guess you're just gonna have to hire some help, old man.
HANK: (*Slamming his fists*) Now just who're you callin' old man, old woman?
DORIS: That grumpy, shriveled up raisin sittin' down at the table, that's who.

The rest of the scene escalates into an argument that mirrors the actual storm coming in. The overheard quote of "Weather man says a storm's comin' in" has been turned into a metaphor for the couple's relationship. The conflict is eventually resolved later in the scene with Hank giving in to his wife and finding someone to help him with the chores around the farm.

The next piece is also written by the same young playwright.

"Nothing more to say"
First Draft

Overheard quote dialogue piece by Lakshami

Characters
LOUISA
JASON

Setting: An apartment

LOUISA: (*Packing a suitcase*) I can't live like this.
JASON: You have for years! How can you suddenly decide that you can't do this anymore?
LOUISA: Because it's my right. It's my decision. I'm part of this too, Jason . . . oh wait. You wouldn't know, would you? You're never around!

JASON: I work, Louisa! How the hell do you think we can afford to live?

LOUISA: Yes. Yes, you work so hard. But, at what cost? (*She shuts the suitcase*)

JASON: So that's it. Nothing more to say?

LOUISA: (*Pauses as she looks at him hoping for more. Pause. She picks up the suitcase and leaves*)

JASON: If you want to live, you'll give me that suitcase.

In this scene the playwright uses the line "Nothing more to say" to epitomize a relationship that has ended. Instead of using it to begin her scene, Lakshami embeds it in the middle of the scene. Ending the scene with a threat raises the stakes.

These dialogues are read aloud in class. Critiques are given and rewrites are done. When we have finished one round of reading, critiquing, and rewriting, I change directions. What if a character in a play overhears something she shouldn't? What kinds of problems would present themselves? Can you think of any plays in which this happens? Can you use any of the overheard phrases on our list for this exercise? The students chose the following phrases:

- "No drugs in school, Joey"
- "She doesn't trust me"
- "Do you think he knows?"

After a quick discussion, I ask the students to write a dialogue between two people. These two people are onstage and talking about something that involves a third person. Person Three is also onstage but cannot be seen by the other two. After the dialogue, Person Three comes forward onstage and delivers a monologue, also written by the student, about what he's overhead and what he is going to do about it. This writing assignment should be three pages in length; two pages of dialogue and one page of monologue.

Another variation is to have Person Three walk onstage in the middle of the dialogue. He overhears only part of the conversation and misunderstands it. Then Person Three delivers the monologue based on the wrongly interpreted information.

You can carry this assignment a step further and improvise a scene in which Person Three is confronted by the two others with the truth and the misunderstanding is settled.

All of this "playing around" can lead to the creation of possible scenarios that the students might want to explore in longer versions, perhaps a ten-minute play or even a one act. As the playwriting class progresses and the students' short pieces grow, they develop in their journals many resources for future playwriting assignments.

Overheard . . . Noises

Overheard conversations are rich resources for writing ideas. Sometimes overheard noises can also be the source of an idea for a play. For example, one day I was making copies for my classes in the school office. Carol, the administrative assistant, was running another printer in the adjacent office and the two machines set up a crazy rhythm. As the copies spewed out, I began to realize I was moving in time to the two rhythms. Carol noticed my "dance" and we began to talk about the crazy "copier song" we were hearing. I told her that someday I would write a play using the overheard noise of the copy machines and Carol said, "You'd better dedicate it to me."

So, to prove that not only can overheard phrases and conversations be an inspiration for playwriting, I share with you a noise-inspired play: "The Drama of Reproduction," dedicated to my copying cohort, Carol. This play actually began as a poem and won second place in a Writer Online contest. The theme of the contest was to write something that depicted *frenzy.* I have since rewritten it as the very short play that follows.

The Drama of Reproduction

A short, almost wordless, play by Maureen Brady Johnson

Characters

MAN
WOMAN
COPY MACHINE (OR CARDBOARD FACSIMILE OF)
FAX MACHINE
DOT MATRIX PRINTER
EPSON STYLUS PRINTER

Setting

Copy machine, down center
Fax machine, up left
Epson Stylus printer, up center
Dot matrix printer, up right
The FAX and PRINTERS are on tables.
An empty table is also onstage.

At Rise: *Stage is dark.*

Spotlight Stage Right
A MAN clothed in a suitcoat, tie, and tights
Spotlight Stage Left
A WOMAN in a blazer and tutu
Spotlight Center Stage
A COPY MACHINE
A measured rhythm begins. Trays fill. Reproduction.

MAN and WOMAN move in place, ever so slightly, to the rhythm.
Then WOMAN moves efficiently and gracefully to retrieve copies and put them in neat little piles on the table.
She "dances" with precision as she brings the paper to the table.
She celebrates order.
She indicates that MAN should help her with this task.
He follows dutifully, taking paper from WOMAN, imitating her movement, and placing it in the neat little piles on the table.
After a minute, he grows weary of the measured pace.

MAN leaps into the air executing a perfect jeté.
WOMAN indicates momentary delight and then returns to her measured pace.

MAN moves Upstage Left, Center and Right where three printers are located.
He turns on a DOT MATRIX, a FAX, and an EPSON STYLUS PRINTER.

He takes a moment to move to the new sounds of the printers. The rhythm rises and falls, each machine's noise adds a bit of madness to the scene and to his "dance."

He celebrates chaos.
He tempts WOMAN to join him.
WOMAN shoots a look at MAN.
He does a lovely pirouette, looks at her and shrugs his shoulders.
He extends his hand for her to abandon the neat little piles and join him.
She refuses.
He shrugs again and continues to celebrate the noisy rhythm.
She runs gracefully, grabbing copies from the DOT MATRIX, the FAX, and the EPSON STYLUS. Stage Right, Center, and Left.
She realizes that there is too much for one person to do.
She indicates to MAN that order must be maintained.
He sighs, follows her, tries to help, realizes the futility, disturbs the neat little piles she is making, slowly at first, building to a point where he is flinging the papers into the air, giving himself over to wild paper abandon.

He celebrates chaos in a joyful "dance."

The rhythm of the machines increases. Sound rises, trays overflow, copies spew, Stage Right, Center, and Left.

She is still committed to sustaining order.
Her pace quickens as she runs from machine to table trying to keep the neat little piles.
MAN and WOMAN pas de deux in frantic conflicting objectives
She grabbing, sorting, piling
He grabbing, dashing, flinging
Until
She realizes (she does not say this aloud) "Oh. What the heck"
She gives herself over to wild paper abandon.
Through a storm of paper coming from above, they complete a liquid, twisting "dance"
and just as they reach for each other . . .
The machines jam.
Silence. BLACKOUT. Spotlight Center Stage
MAN and WOMAN look into each other's eyes
PAUSE
and say, "You do have the original?" BLACKOUT. The End.

In Summary

My students continued to write random, overheard phrases in their journals for the rest of the semester. These phrases were used as titles and themes for plays, opening lines for characters, and as inspiration for class scene work. There were days when I'd show up for class and two or three phrases were written on the board with two or three students asking us to begin our day's writing assignment with their quotes.

"I heard this today in the student commons."
"I heard this at the town meeting."
"Mr. Michael said this in philosophy class today."
"Can we use it today for scene work?"

My answer: "Sure. Let's get to work."

On days like this, I smile, realizing that I'm not the only one who sees the haiku dancing in the air.

4 Inspired by a Song

Someday I'm going to write a play about a woman who hears a series of songs from her past and is instantly thrown back to the place, memory, and moment of the first time she heard it. The set changes would probably be impossible, but think "Walter Mitty." I don't know whether it will be a comedy or a tragedy, but it will address the power of music and its ability to alter place and time.

I can be driving in a car and an old Beatles song comes on and I am instantly taken back to junior high and a babysitting job that was horrible to endure. I took the babysitting job to earn the last three dollars to buy the Beatles 1965 record and I would bear anything to get that album.

My husband and I have "our songs." Corny as it sounds, when we hear Ed Ames singing "My Cup Runneth Over with Love," we are in each other's arms dancing to the first song at our wedding reception, awash in the very same emotions we were feeling thirty-plus years ago. I know that we are not alone in experiencing this phenomenon. Music has extraordinary power.

My dad used to kid me about my music when I was growing up. He'd ask, "What kind of love songs are you going to have to remember?" But my dad knew how much I needed my music. He fixed the

Hi-Fi when it was expensive to repair because I needed to sit in the dark with a broken heart, crying and listening to Dionne Warwick. He understood the power that music, even *my* music, had to heal.

Today, music is one of the most powerful forces in our students' lives. The class of 2008 at Duke University will receive a free iPod to use for their classes. I would venture to say that in addition to their academic use, those iPods will have a lot of music on them.

My students are passionate about their music. They talk about it, analyze it, move to it, and watch video interpretations of it. Music is as much of an inspiration to them as it was to my generation. How could I channel this passion and use it as an inspiration for playwriting? After all, plays bend time and place just like music.

Using music as a source of inspiration for playwriting is one of the most successful exercises I've ever tried. I begin by sharing two or three songs that mean something to me. I try to choose two songs from the past and one song that is more current. It is a risk-taking experience for an instructor to do this, but it models the behavior you want the students to imitate when it is their turn to share. If you are willing to take some risks in class then they will, too. If they believe that they can take risks by sharing their music, then they will take risks as playwrights. And no play is written without taking many risks.

You don't have to share more than one song. Time may not allow it. Even the explanation of what the song means to you can be brief. The important things to share are

- where and when you heard it, and
- who was involved in the memory.

For example, one year I chose "Scarborough Fair" by Simon and Garfunkle, "Winter" by Tori Amos, and "Superman" by Five for Fighting. I shared with my students the time I sang "Scarborough Fair" in a coffeehouse in high school at the height of the Vietnam War. Some of my friends were going to be drafted when they completed high school. When I sang that song, I was thinking of their lives and it was overwhelmingly sad. "Winter" was a song my daughters shared with me. They made me a mix tape and I'd listen to it in the car while driving them back and forth to school events. Whenever I hear the song I think of how fast they grew up and how things change as they do. "Superman" is my 9–11 song. It is connected to that terrible day when everyone realized how vulnerable we all are just like the superhero in the song. It epitomizes the helplessness I felt that day as the entire school gathered in our commons area to watch what unfolded throughout the morning and into the afternoon on TV. Life was filled with supermen and women that day. Yet, we realized the frailty of superheroes. These three songs have the power to transport me to three different and significant time periods in my life.

I ask the students to bring to the next class a song that sends them to a different time and place. If you want songs without expletives, tell your students *before* they bring in such a piece. Emphasize that what you are looking for is the meaning that the song gives to their lives. It should take them back in time and memory. Just to reinforce the seriousness of this assignment, I assign a short writing piece as homework (see the form in the Appendix, page 119). The students should answer the following questions:

- Why is this one of your favorite songs? Be specific.
- Where and when did you hear the song for the first time?
- What memories does this song bring to mind?
- Is there a particular phrase or part of a lyric that really resonates with you? Include these phrases at the end of your essay.

For the next two classes, we listen to the songs and the students' explanations of why they like them. Each student should play the song first and then read their essay aloud. The biggest problem is keeping the students on track discussing the points in their essays. The discussions can splinter into a wide variety of conversations about music in general and musicians in particular. Be prepared to bring the discussion back to the real reason you are doing this, namely, to inspire a short scene or play.

Scene Writing from a Lyric

The next writing assignment involves taking one of the phrases the student has chosen from their song and using it as the theme of a five-minute scene. As a class, we first work together with one phrase so that I can show them what I am looking for in this assignment.

This prep work saves a lot of time. Any questions the students have are answered along the way.

For this part of the exercise, the teacher can use one of the songs she shared with the class and a favorite lyric from that song. I used a song that my daughter, Erin, had written called, "Pictures of You." I play the song for the class and then pull a lyric out of the song to use for the writing exercise. I write the phrase ". . . I saw you in every face I passed on the street" on the board. We brainstorm as a class as to what kind of scene could be written with this phrase as its theme. We talk about what kinds of characters, conflict, and resolution would be possible. Some of the ideas that came up were:

- A comedy scene where the main character actually sees the face of his mom or boss or significant other who has been causing some stress in his life.
- A scene about a girl whose boyfriend just broke up with her.
- A scene about a ghost face that keeps appearing on people's faces as they try to renovate a house where a murder has been committed.

The students must understand that the quote they pull from their song is the theme of the scene. They are not reproducing the story in the song. They're making an intellectual leap from song to favorite lyric to the theme of the play. Another example would be the phrase ". . . all you hide from everyone." The ideas that the students brainstormed were:

- A scene between a model who secretly wants to begin a career as an actor and his agent.
- A comedy scene about a kleptomaniac.
- A burn victim, whose wounds are hidden beneath his clothing, falls in love.

After working on these two examples, your students should get the point of using a quote from their favorite song for the next individual writing assignment. The following plays were written by students in response to this assignment.

Marissa's piece was inspired by one of her favorite songs, "You're Not Alone" by Amy Grant. It was performed as part of our evening of original plays. The audience loved this piece. Marissa worked on the play throughout the year, adding different scenes, writing, rewriting, and polishing until she came up with a draft that she could see being performed. The rewrite was included the following year as part of our evening of one acts. This scene was part of several scenes making up her one act entitled, "The Norm."

Anna Invisible

by Marissa

Characters

ANNA	BETTY
CARL	BELINDA
BETH	BARBIE
MAX	FRAN
BRITTNEY	ARNOLD

Setting: Outside of a school

At Rise: *There are several bunches of distinct groups of teenage kids eating lunch at different picnic tables outside of a school.* ANNA *is sitting at a table by herself saying "hi" to people as they pass. They ignore her.*

ANNA: Hi Susie, nice job in the play last week . . . Hi Gracie! . . . Hi Paul. Oh, hi Carl

ANNA *gets up and starts walking toward* CARL, *who is sitting with* BETH.

ANNA: Hi, Carl, ready for your debate tournament this Friday?

CARL *ignores* ANNA.

CARL: Don't take it personally, Beth, but you're totally wrong. You see people aren't born with a personality, you gradually build one as you grow up.

ANNA *comes and sits down at the table where* CARL *and* BETH *are sitting.*

BETH: Genetics has something to do with it as well. I mean, if you're born really ugly, you may end up being very shy and sitting at the shy people table, *but* if you're born with a very athletic build, you'll be good at sports and sit at the jock table . . .

CARL: Yes, but if that athletic person was brought up playing the piano, and *not* sports, he'd be sitting at the music geek table.

BETH: That's possible, *but* don't you think someone who had a better body type for one activity would lean toward doing that one thing?

ANNA: Don't you two think it could be a combination of genetics and surroundings?

BETH *and* CARL *look at* ANNA *and then back at each other, and continue to talk as if they had not heard her.*

CARL: It isn't all genetics.

BETH: But it can't be all upbringing.

CARL: Maybe it's a combination of both.

BETH: Yeah, that must be it.

CARL *and* BETH *are not listening.*

BETH: (*To Anna*) What? Did you say something?

ANNA: No, no. Nothing.

ANNA *gets up and moves to the jock table.*

MAX: Hey, go long!

BRETT *gets up from the table and goes long to catch the football being thrown by* MAX.

BRITTNEY: (*Brittney is talking to the group of cheerleaders*) So, I told him, like oh my God, no. Who do *you* think you are telling me I wear too much makeup?! Like, who made you Mr. Cosmetics?

BETTY: So, did you like dump him again or something?

BRITTNEY: Yeah, but he brought me a teddy bear the next day, so we're back together again!

BELINDA: That is so cute!

BARBIE: Totally adorable!

BRITTNEY: I know.

BRITTNEY *takes the teddy bear out of her bag and shows the cheerleaders.*

ALL CHEERLEADERS: Ahhh.

ANNA: Hi, Brittney!

BRITTNEY: Oh, hi . . . uhm . . . uhm.

BARBIE *whispers* ANNA'S *name to* BRITTNEY.

BRITTNEY: Anna.

The CHEERLEADERS *begin to talk among themselves.*

ANNA: I really like that blouse. Isn't it from the Nicolette clothing line?

No one responds to ANNA's remark.

BETTY: I really like that top Brittney.

BELINDA: Yeah, wherever did you find it?

BARBIE: It's absolutely fab.

BRITTNEY: Oh, it's the new line of clothing by Nicolette, special order. It's just to die for.

ANNA: (*Anna gets up from the jock table*) Bye.

No one answers her. They are too busy talking. ANNA *moves to the dork table and sits down.*

FRAN: So, so, the liquid then goes into the gaseous state because the molecules are moving sooooo fast they get really excited. Hah, hah, isn't that neato?

ARNOLD: And, and when the molecules slow way, way down, they go into solid state!

FRAN: Totally awesome!

ANNA: Don't the molecules slow way down when they get cold?

FRAN *and* ARNOLD *don't hear* ANNA.

FRAN: Super awesome! Let's go to the science lab!

ANNA: And when the molecules get faster, it's because they were heated, right?

Again, they don't hear ANNA.

ARNOLD: Yeah, let's go right now!

ARNOLD *and* FRAN *exit and* ANNA *is left sitting alone at the table watching other kids pass by. Everyone walks by* ANNA *and exits off stage, not noticing her as she speaks.*

ANNA: Hi Sammy! Hi Sara, how's your cold? Hi Charlie, did you win the chess tournament? Scott!! Great touchdown last Friday!

The lunch bell rings and everyone exits except ANNA. *She is alone onstage. The sound and lights slowly fade during speech.*

ANNA: Hi Dexter! Come sit down. How was the swim meet last week? You placed second! That's great! Oh, my week was fine. Had my driving lessons. They kinda stink but I really want my license soon. Oh, you already took them? I'm glad the written test wasn't too hard. I've been worrying about it. Oh, don't go Dexter, you can be a little late for your next class, can't you? You can sit right here next to me and we can talk. We can talk about school, and swimming . . . and driving . . . and the trip to the Grand Canyon we took last summer . . . and all sorts of things.

ANNA *continues talking. Blackout.*

ANNA: . . . and the new motorboat . . . school dances . . . friends . . .
The End

Variation

A variation on this assignment is to ask students to remember the first time they heard the song. Ask them to write a scene capturing the moment they first heard the song. If they can't remember every detail, they should use their imagination.

One student, Georgia, opens her scene in the family car. They are traveling cross-country and the family is moving for the third time in her short life.

"Do RE Me" by Georgia

The first time I heard "Do Re Me," I was crouched in the front seat of the jeep with my window down so the cold air could stain my face. You could feel the vibration of the music, as well as every bump on the road. We were on our way to California, the Paradise State. Soon, we were to realize that this statement was nothing but false.

Another student, Stacey, remembers a time when she and a friend were jumping on the bed as they sang the song. They were jumping and leaping and heard a loud crack. The incident ends with a broken bed and the two youngsters sheepishly admitting to their parents that "Livin' La Vida Loca" was the cause of the accident.

You can also use this assignment to concentrate on other elements of playwriting. Sometimes I ask the students to concentrate on creating a mood or setting a tone with their scenes. This mood or tone should imitate the mood or tone that is created when the song is played. This worked very well when one of my students wrote a piece called "The Day the Towers Fell." It was his way of coping with the tragedy of 9–11. He used the song I had played in class, "Superman" by Five for Fighting, as inspiration.

The music he chose set the tone and the mood of the scene. Not only did he use a lyric from the song to inspire the theme, but he used the poignant quality of the song itself to convey the feeling of his scene. When it was performed for an audience, he used a smoke machine. When all of these elements came together onstage, it made quite an impact.

The Day the Towers Fell

A scene for two actors

by Jonathan

Characters

ELIJAH MARTIN A homeless man in New York; essentially lives out of his prized trench coat. A former college student down on his luck; tends to chronicle his thoughts on a portable tape recorder. He's in his late twenties or thirties.

KID Comes from a well-off family, dressed in a private school uniform; frantically searching for his parents, both of whom were at the World Trade Center. He's fifteen years old—between child and adult.

Setting: A bench in a deserted park in Manhattan

Time: September 11, 2001, three o'clock in the afternoon—just hours after the attack at the World Trade Center

A bench in a deserted New York City park. Enter ELIJAH, *a homeless man. He has slung over his shoulder a ragged trench coat. He collapses onto the park bench; he takes the coat and puts it on.*

ELIJAH: (*As he puts the coat on*) Damn . . . (*He reaches into the pocket of his jeans and takes out an minature tape recorder; he clicks it on*)

ELIJAH: September 11—'bout three. Found it right where I left it. Cops didn't notice me. (*Beat*) To bring things up to date—took off my coat 'cause it was hot, right before the Towers got hit. Lay low for a few hours before I went back for it. Was right where I left it. Looks like everything's still in it, too.

From his pocket, he fishes out a half-crushed packet of Chips-Ahoy cookies. He rips open the packet and starts to eat. He doesn't notice the kid—who enters; like ELIJAH, *he's covered with soot.*

ELIJAH: (*Eating*) Must've been maybe a couple hundred people at ground zero when I slipped back in . . . Hiroshima in the middle of Manhattan. Ash hung so thick in the air I could barely see in front of me . . .

KID: Hey! (*Startled, Elijah looks up*) Hey—you've been to the site?

ELIJAH: What?

KID: Have you been to the bomb site?

ELIJAH: (*Hesitant*) Uhh . . . yeah.

KID: (*Frantic*) Hey, look . . . hold on (*He searches through his pockets*)

ELIJAH: (*Eyes him warily. Kid finally pulls out a crumpled photograph*)

KID: (*Holds out photo*) Did you see this guy? Anyone who looked like this guy?

ELIJAH: (*Stares at photograph*) Kid, I don't know. (*Kid collapses onto the bench*) Maybe I did—thing is, you can barely see three feet in there. And everyone's wearing masks . . .

KID: F**k. (*Starts to cry—repeats the word over and over again, like a mantra*)

ELIJAH: (*Pause. He's not sure what to do*) Can I see that again?

Kid doesn't respond—just keeps crying. ELIJAH *pulls the photo out of his hand.*

ELIJAH: This your dad? (*Kid doesn't stop crying, but nods his head*) What about your mom?

KID: Visiting him.
ELIJAH: Did you show this to a cop?
KID: (*Nods*)
ELIJAH: Did they see them?

The next few minutes of the play are spent in a conversation about the whereabouts of the parents of the young student. Elijah must decide whether to help Kid search for his parents or leave him to fend for himself. A symbolic gesture with the significant object, the trench coat, follows and the play ends.

ELIJAH: Here. (*The Kid takes the handkerchief and wipes off his face, blows his nose. He stands up. Elijah takes off his trench coat*) Put this on. Tuck up the collar—keeps the dust from getting in. (*The Kid does so. Elijah pulls his t-shirt up around his mouth*) This way.

They walk offstage. As they do so, ELIJAH'S *tape recorder slips out of the trench coat's pocket. It falls on the ground. As they leave, it begins to play, as the lights fade.*

ELIJAH: (*Recorded voice coming from the tape recorder*)
—ember fifth, eight in the morning. I've realized something about New York—all the steel around here does something to the mind. Makes it feel cold, invincible—as high and mighty as a skyscraper. That's the Manhattan mindset—everything here is frozen and proud, from the colleges to the people. Yeah, that's NYC—a metal Babylon, population six million and a half . . . psychological Towers of Babel . . .

The recording fades with the lights, and eventually is gone.

The End

A Word About Performances

Aside from reading their works in class, I have two other methods of getting my playwriting kids' scenes in front of an audience: "Ten at Eleven and a Half" and "Give Me the Works."

"Ten at Eleven and a Half" is a lunchtime performance. My acting students take the first drafts from the playwrights and they read through the scenes a few times. Then, at lunch we invite the school to come to the Black Box Theatre to see a staged reading of two or three scenes. The audience eats their lunch while watching the readings. The young playwrights hear the audience's reaction to the first draft plays or scene. The performers give the playwrights a chance to hear how the dialogue holds together and after the readings, the audience gives a written critique (see form on page 120) to the playwrights to help them with their rewrites. I also give a cookie to every audience member who hands in a critique. A little bribery, but it really works!

If you don't have any acting students to help out like this, you could enlist the aid of your faculty members. You might even want to take the best plays and scenes written in a semester and have an evening performance.

"Give Me the Works" is the title of our evening of original theatre and, other than "NightScene," which is our evening of student-directed scenes, "Give Me the Works" is the most popular show of the year. I think one of the reasons is because of the ownership the young playwrights have over the material. I also think that their classmates want to see what the playwrights feel is important enough to write about.

No matter how you provide your young playwrights with a chance to see and hear their work, it is absolutely essential that you do. Whether it is a simple dramatic read-through during class or a full-blown production complete with smoke machines, it is necessary to the rewriting process. If you allow your playwrights to keep everything in their head and never risk seeing their scenes performed, you are eliminating one of the most important elements in theatre: the audience.

As I have said before, this unit is particularly popular with my students. I've had more fine work created using music as an inspiration than almost any other unit. Some of their work appears earlier in this chapter. In those pieces, the themes were inspired by the lyric of a favorite song. One of the variations of this unit is to have the students write about the first time they heard their favorite song. The short piece that follows is a monologue-type vignette that explores the first time this student, Brian, heard a particular song.

The Summer of Dreams
by Brian

Normally, I wouldn't drive to Shaker. In retrospect, it's a place that I would like to forget. Like the paint on my arms, that summer will stain me for a while. I was a painter. My pallette was not a 12 × 36 piece of paper. My canvas was an entire house. Yes, I was a liquids application engineer whose soul purpose was to apply liquid solvents to augment and ameliorate the appearance of selected domiciles. Statements like this make me feel that I was more important than I actually was.

Being a house painter was easily the worst job I ever had. The first day of work was characterized by waking up early. This wasn't bad since I started the day after school let out. So sleeping in wasn't really a habit I had to break.

When they first dispatched us to Shaker, I went with my project manager in his 1989 extension van, replete with faded red interior and that stench that screams grandma.

The longer the trip took, the slower the time went. It was so bad that I started daydreaming. The entire time I was hoping for two small things. The first was for 2 Mig 21-Russian fighter planes to swoop down, and simultaneously napalm and cluster bomb I-490.

The second thing was for us to get lost. I'm not talking about turning left when you're supposed to go straight. I'm talking about being lost in biblical proportions; Lake Erie parting, and us wandering around in Canada for some random amount of time that adds up to 40. At the time when God was giving me Canadian bacon, instead of manna, my fantasy was interrupted like hearing a cat fall 50 ft from your friend's roof.

The song that came onto the radio was the pinnacle of American pop music. Loud, annoying and out of key. As the first few notes rang proudly through the air like nails on a chalkboard, my project manager gave a yelp like a thirteen-year-old girl getting makeup for the first time. To muffle out his feminine shriek, he turned up the music.

Instantly God, bacon, Canaan, or Canada vanished. As the fighter jets swooped down, a sidewinder missile struck a nearby light pole. It burst into thousands of pieces going every which way, which actually reminded me of that time when Uncle Randy knocked over the entire jar of bottle rockets. Nevertheless, with my fantasy still intact, I made sure that a piece of shrapnel went through the radio. I could tell from then on that I was going to have one memorable summer.

I really love the subtle humor in Brian's piece. I especially like the fact that his music memory is not a pleasant one but it still works as a monologue. Later in the semester, his scenes and short plays grew using a blend of comedy and sadness.

Bending Time and Space

Music and drama have the power to bend time and space. I know exactly where I'll be inside my head when I hear a Beatles song. The images and characters it conjures up can sit there inside my brain or I can let them out. Sometimes I quietly savor the thoughts but there are other times when the memory is too strong to stay inside my head. So, I let it out in a scene or a play.

Our students feel just as passionately about their music as we do about ours. Using this passion to inspire a new character or scene or even a full-length play makes so much sense. Even though, like my dad, I might not understand the songs, I'll look forward to the plays that they inspire.

A Pile of Junk . . . a Piece of Theatre

I was in a rush one morning to get to school. As I opened my dresser drawer to find a pair of scissors, a vintage Captain Hook puppet for my son's upcoming birthday fell to the floor. I picked it up and placed it next to a lacquered jewelry box from China. Then, I took a minute to pause and take a good look at the top of my dresser. The Captain Hook puppet was lying next to the jewelry box, which was next to a statue of Jesus, a jellyfish puppet, a bottle of Advil, a spool of thread, Chapstick, some spray perfume, and a framed card from my husband. Instead of saying to myself, "It's time to clean off my dresser," I said, "This is the weirdest juxtaposition of stuff I have ever seen. I think I'll take a picture of it." After I took the picture, I did say to myself, "It's time to clean off the dresser." But not before I hatched another idea for playwriting. These objects on my dresser had meaning to me. They represented pieces of my life. This meaning was lost on the average person. Writing about the relationship between these random objects and my life would be a great exercise to strengthen such writing skills as:

- Giving meaning to dissimilar things
- Using dissimilarities to create conflict
- Transferring these ideas to show how relationships develop between people who have dissimilarities

A play takes us on a journey through unrelated events and the playwright gives them meaning. I could ask my students to create a collage of dissimilar things that they own and value, take a photograph of it, and write a monologue explaining their relationship to this odd mixture of grouped images. They could share the picture and the monologue with the class. Then, using the monologue and the picture as foundation, they could create a short scene. This scene would use the students' objects and show the importance of these objects to two or three student-created characters. They would introduce conflict into the scene centering around the objects. If the students could establish a relationship between characters and these dissimilar objects, they might begin to explore the idea of relationships between dissimilar characters and their different wants and needs.

As preparation for this writing assignment, I wanted to begin with something simple. I began taking photographs of two unrelated objects. I was surprised that I didn't have to "set up" these pictures. I just looked around my everyday life, found them, and photographed them.

Over a period of a few weeks I photographed:

- a llama rocker that someone had put out in the trash
- a single boxing glove decorated with the American flag lying in the street by the curb
- a toaster on the entrance ramp of a highway
- a coffee pot on the grass at a school crossing
- a foam cup wedged in the branches of a tree
- a window at an ice cream stand with a sign reading: *Please do not set children on the counter.*
- a rusted swing set with weeds grown up all around it

For our first class, I asked the students to look at the photos. They passed the pictures around the room. Then I asked them to brainstorm by answering the questions:

- How did that object get there?
- Who put it there? Why did they put it there?
- In what ways are these objects similar? Dissimilar?
- Can you figure out a relationship between the objects?

These questions can be found on a form in the Appendix, page 121. During the brainstorming sessions, three pictures drew a lot of attention. The coffee cup wedged in the tree received a lot of comments.

"Maybe someone wanted to keep their coffee safe while they were working outside."

"Maybe they forgot they put it there."

"Maybe some birds built a nest in it."

I asked the students, "Can you see any conflict created by the juxtaposition of these two objects?"

"Maybe the maintenance crew came along and a big argument started. One of them wanted to throw the cup away. Another person wants to leave the cup because of the bird's nest."

"Maybe someone put the cup in the tree to hide the fact that they were drinking coffee. They saw someone coming who knew that they weren't supposed to be drinking it and the scene takes place with the coffee drinker trying to keep the cup in a tree a secret."

The llama rocker in the trash was another popular photo. The discussion went something like this:

"There's a sign next to it that says *free.* Why didn't anyone take it?"

"Who would throw such an unusual piece away?"

"Maybe a kid was going away to college and his parents want him to get rid of his childhood stuff."

"Maybe the kid doesn't want to get rid of it. The parents smuggle it out to the curb and the kid comes home and finds it and gets angry."

"Or he finds it and tries to smuggle it back into the house."

"Or the parents try to get rid of it and put it out on the curb. The kid finds out and he is just about to smuggle it back into the house and the little girl from next door comes by and the kid ends up giving the llama rocker to her."

As the brainstorming sessions continued, the students began to draw their own conclusions and create their own characters with conflicting objectives. The photos with two dissimilar objects forced the students to think. The photos challenged their ability to figure out the puzzle that was present with a juxtaposition of objects. Then I asked the students to choose one of these photographs and write a monologue.

One of the students asked to use the picture of the boxing glove with the American flag on it in the ditch by a curb. The following excerpted piece is a first draft monologue of what the picture inspired.

America's War Thrown to the Curb

by Russ

The War.
The cause sold as a lie to bring a voice to a silenced crowd.
To bring order to chaos.
"The people will welcome us," they said.
"Our morals should be theirs," they said.
"The inevitable rules of uncertainty and entropy will yield to us," they said. "Our essence, our freedom is at stake," they said.
Well, let me tell you something. I am tired of your greed. I am tired of your warped view of what we are and how I should live. . . .
I beg you to leave my world. Exit my dream. I am tired of you. . . .
Let me be . . . without you . . .

Another student, Aaron, took one of my photographs home with him. It was a picture of an ice cream stand with a sign on the window, *Please do not set children on the counter.* The excerpted piece that follows has a darkly humorous event at its heart. It also held many possibilities for future scenes and conflicts among the child, his friend, and the parents who left him behind.

The Awkward Sign

by Aaron

The sign was there when I was young. But my parents obviously didn't see it. I blocked it as they set me down. At least they gave me ice cream before they forgot me there. Or left me on purpose, I suppose. I grew up without them. I didn't really know until I was twelve. . . . One kid asked me why my parents had done this. I had no idea why they didn't see the sign that said: *Please do not set children on the counter.*

Stacey used the photo of a rusted swing set with weeds growing all around it for her assignment. She immediately assumed that a father had neglected the yard, the swing set, and his family. The possibilities for character creation and conflict are many and varied. This piece was a good start.

The Swing Set

by Stacey

> You see, he never did anything for us. It's not like he could, though. I didn't meet him until the day after he came home, the day he bought us that swing set. It was red and white. He put it together in our backyard. I was so excited. All the other kids had wooden swing sets. They got splinters. But ours was metal and shiny and new. I was happy that my father came home. He smiled, but it was a fake smile. I was afraid to look at him. His eyes were hazed over with a dark despair.

One of my more creative students, Laura, went home that same day and made her own picture of dissimilar objects. She assembled random parts of a medieval costume that she had made. She added a mask and a mirror to the arrangement and took a digital picture of the collage. Then she wrote the following piece. This short poem alludes to a relationship that is fraught with intrigue and mystery. The resulting play would capitalize on this relationship and the image of empty eyes.

Remnants

by Laura

Black feathers on Crimson
And sharp on smooth
The empty eyes staring at you
Remnants of the past
An age of silk and fans
Of daggers and intrigue
The empty eyes staring at you.

Using Visual Images to Inspire Young Playwrights

This exercise can be challenging to both students and instructors. The photographs of juxtaposed objects can stretch any imagination. Taking pictures of random dissimilar objects can be "set up" or can be discovered in our everyday lives. I had a lot of fun just looking around my neighborhood and snapping pictures of odd and eccentric things. Once you begin looking for such pictures, objects certainly present themselves. I found that in doing this exercise, my sensitivity to the random juxtaposition of objects we encounter in everyday life increased immensely.

Trying to show a relationship between dissimilar objects is a natural lead-in to writing about relationships between dissimilar characters. Crafting a play brings dissimilar emotions to life, side by side, in scene after scene. Characters that are dissimilar create conflict. They need to want different things to create conflict. This exercise helps the students to recognize this in the everyday objects around them.

A Larger-Than-Life Production

One year, I used a large assortment of unrelated objects to inspire a playwriting and performing project. The process took place during four days, using five hours a day. At the end of our school year, we are given a block of time to do group projects with our students. The experience can also be broken down into class periods and used during the school year. It was a visceral, hands-on experience for my playwrights and performers. It took a lot of prep work, but it was well worth it. The following section discusses an idea from an article published in the Fall of 1997 in *Teaching Theatre.*

In conventional theatre productions the director follows a series of steps. She chooses the script (step one). She meets with the team, which includes a set designer, to discuss her concept for the production (step two). She auditions the performers (step three), begins rehearsal (step four), and oversees the construction of the set (step five) until it all comes together in a final production.

What if these steps were rearranged? What if the director began with the construction of a huge, sculptural set piece that inspired the playwrights to write and then perform these writings around the sculpture/set pieces? I thought it would be an interesting project to attempt. During a stretch of four days (five hours each) a group of students, an art teacher, and I glued, stapled, caulked, improvised, wrote, revised, and performed around a huge set piece of our own creation. This project proved that when you approach theatre in a unique and imaginative way, anything can and does happen.

In preparation for the project, we needed materials. The first step was to collect junk from a wide variety of sources. We went to lumber companies and asked for donated scraps and end pieces of wood. We transported a van full of large cardboard rings from a stamping plant. An excavation company donated pieces of huge plastic sewer pipe and multicolored drainage pipes. We got permission to crawl around dumpsters at construction sites and found bendable scraps of aluminum. We cleaned out the school's pole barn and found old animal cages and exercise equipment. The students contributed things like old telephones, hubcaps, and bolts of fabric. We bought floating pool noodles, spray foam insulation, spray paint, and glue.

Step two was to dump all of this stuff onstage and let the students take a look at it. We walked around picking our way among the incredibly dissimilar junk. Then small groups of students gravitated toward certain things. They began to select objects from the pile of junk we had onstage and work together to connect the pieces. They dragged, pulled, piled, and wired stuff together. They hot glued, spray painted, and then changed their minds and pulled certain creations apart and then put them back together again in a whole new configuration. Some students took all day painting and hot gluing small objects to other small objects. Some students climbed all over the biggest objects they could find and created mammoth pieces that they could stand on. After one day's work we had a set piece that took up two-thirds of the stage.

As the students worked in separate groups, the art teacher and I circulated around the activity to help. We critiqued pieces for their stability; we offered suggestions on possible areas on which to concentrate and gave practical advice on how to attach things to other things.

A couple of students took one of the animal cages and a can of spray insulation foam and worked outside. They dribbled the foam on the cage and the effect was startling. The dribbled material looked like yellow blobs of some alien material. In the performance, the students used the set piece as a symbol of feeling trapped and ultimately, freed.

Another group took some of the aluminum and bent it into a stick man shape. They paired this up with the pool noodles and hung it from the ceiling of the theatre. The entire sculpture slowly twisted and turned as the air conditioning unit came on and off. It became a huge mobile.

Some students took the pipes and glued them together making a long tube that looked like it was emptying onstage. Eventually they would use it as a giant megaphone in our performance pieces.

Another student used a bunch of plastic frames as a hiding place by gluing them together in a tower. In performance she hid in the tower only to enter the playing area by popping out of the tower to surprise the audience.

As the set pieces took shape, we would take time out from our construction work to look at the massive "mess" and write. We began this third step in the process by moving away from the stage and viewing the sculpture as a whole. The students would sit and write. Then they walked around the piece, found a place to sit onstage and write something new with their new perspective on the piece. Then the performers got up, moved to a different place and wrote some more. The writings took the form of poetry, monologues, quotations, and short dialogues. Some of the dialogues were *with* the sculpture itself.

As the set piece grew and the young authors wrote, a theme began to emerge. Childhood dreams and nightmares became the central idea for our show. As we assembled the script, it had a definite absurdist, experimental-type feel to it. The students loved it! They asked if we could add some original music composed by one of the students. They also wanted to add sound effects and noise to the performance. Someone offered to bring in their keyboard.

The script assembly took time. I let them give their opinion as to how the show was to be put together but I did tell them up front I would let them know when I didn't think the script was working. The script was 95 percent theirs with about 5 percent teacher intervention. It was a student experimental playwriting/performing experience and I wanted to keep it that way. This process produced a master script that was assembled and given to every playwright/performer. The script was thirty-five pages in length.

The final step was putting it together and rehearsing. On day four we had a lot of decisions to make. The students decided that they wanted the audience to sit onstage. We also had to review the music cues and get someone to run the CD player. Some scenes had audience participation and that had to be worked out. Some scenes required more than one actor so those parts had to be cast. I tried to oversee all of this and make sure this production was not becoming a showcase for a few players. We also decided to let the audience explore the set before we began the production. We needed to station performers around the set piece so no damage was done by the audience touching parts of it.

We rehearsed for four hours. It was not a supremely polished piece but it was theirs and it *was* experimental. The usual problems presented themselves during rehearsal; timing, memorization, blocking. But the students had invested so much of themselves in the creation of the set and the play that they really wanted it to work. They compromised on many points.

The whole experience was highly successful. Everyone was challenged to think. Their usual ideas of theatre and playwriting were twisted and bent, like the metal man in the free-floating sculpture onstage! A degree of passionate involvement with set and script was achieved by the students. This passion infected the audience as they watched the production unfold.

As I reflect on the four-day experience, I can see there are things I might have done differently. For example, the original pile of junk materials was too large and perhaps, too random. In the future, I would probably find materials that relate to each other, perhaps by color or texture. I would have liked more time to rehearse, using five full days. It would have been nice to have two performances, one in the afternoon and one in the evening for parents to attend.

In Summary

Rearranging the traditional steps that lead to a production is risky, but the benefits it gives to young playwrights and performers are worth it. Theatre is supposed to shake people up, to challenge their thinking. Shaking up a young playwright by asking him to write about juxtaposing images in a photograph or to create a set of pieces from random, unrelated objects can lead to the "Ah ha" moment we all yearn for when we see a play. As the playwrights look at the juxtaposition of images, they experience the "Ah ha" of discovering relationships. With this visceral experience, it is much easier for them to create such a moment for their audiences as they write.

6 Life . . . on the Rocks

I live in Oberlin, Ohio. It is a college town of incredible beauty, peopled with the most eclectic blend of humanity. There is a town square with a bandstand resembling a Japanese cart, flower beds that bloom from spring into fall, and an assortment of rare and stately trees. Also in this town square, for as long as I have lived here, there are three very large rocks. These rocks are painted regularly with messages ranging from the poignant to the absurd. They advertise productions, celebrate birthdays, and announce the change of seasons. They also splash personal messages to parties unknown. It made me curious to know why a person would want to paint a personal plea for the whole town to see. When "Jon. I'm so sorry" appeared on a rock one day, I decided that there might be a playwriting idea here. I began taking pictures of these messages on the rocks. (Copies of my photos are in the Appendix on pages 110–114 and are on the Heinemann website, www.heinemann.com. They can be copied and used in your classroom.)

I also watched as the rocks were being painted. The groups of people that painted the rocks were as diverse as the messages. I watched as little children stretched to get their paint in the right places. I watched as parents helped them to reach. I watched students paint each other more than the rock. I saw spray paint and house paint used with a wide variety of application styles. It occurred to me that the "blocking" of a play about rock painting was inherently simple, yet challenging. This blocking could give energy and focus to a scene.

After I had about twenty pictures, I formulated the following writing experience for my young playwrights. The students would take a look at my rock message photos and choose one. They would then write a dialogue that took place as the characters painted the rock. During the dialogue, the real story of the message on the rock would come to light.

This would be a challenge to my young playwrights because they would have to think backward. They were looking at the end product when they looked at the rock message. They would have to trace a scene back to the action that leads to the rock being painted. This thinking back through the action gives the students a stronger sense of cause and effect. It gives clarity to a scene. This theory is explained with great detail in *Backwards and Forwards: A Technical Manual for Reading Plays* by David Ball (Southern Illinois University Press, 1983).

With my photographs in hand, I was ready to begin "Life on the Rocks" with my students. I chose five of the best rock pictures and placed them on a table. (You could also pin them up on a board.) The students took some time to look at them and talk about them. Then they asked what we were going to do with them.

I explained the history of the rock messages in Oberlin. I told the students about the times I had seen the rocks being painted. I asked them which pictures appealed to them the most and what would cause a person to write a message on a rock. I asked them if they had a chance to paint a rock, what would they say? We discussed their choices and that discussion led into a brainstorming session about possible scenes that they could write about two characters painting the rock. I asked them to write in their journals three ideas for a possible dialogue, using their favorite photo as inspiration. For homework that night, I asked them to write a first draft of the dialogue.

They knew that they had to build on previous writing assignments that used the following:

- strong characterization
- clear objectives for those characters
- conflict and resolution

The following scenes were written by my students in response to

- the visual stimulus of the picture
- the process of thinking backward
- the activity of painting a huge rock

Ryan's Apology

"Jon. I'm so sorry!"

by Nick

CYRIL: Hey, Ryan whatcha doing?
RYAN: Hey, Cyril. I'm just painting the rock.
CYRIL: At 4:30 in the morning?
RYAN: I have something to say.
CYRIL: (*He reads the rock*) Jon? Why are you writing to Jon?
RYAN: Hey, just let me finish here.
CYRIL: I thought you didn't like him anyway.
RYAN: No. He's OK.
CYRIL: I specifically remember you saying he was a jerk.
RYAN: That was a long time ago.
CYRIL: No, dude. It was yesterday.
RYAN: (*Long pause. Sigh*) You're right.
CYRIL: Dude, what's up with you?
RYAN: I'm fine.
CYRIL: No, you're not. You're all depressed and . . .
RYAN: Well, I got really drunk at this party and um . . .
CYRIL: All right. So far, so good.
RYAN: So I was driving home, still drunk and um, I'm not quite sure how it happened, but one moment I was driving and the next my car was flipped over and um, I crawled out and then I found Jon's car and he was dead.
CYRIL: Oh, f**k.

Communication Rocks

"Jon. I'm so sorry!"

by Amber

ANITA: That was a really stupid argument, anyways.
TINA: Whatever. Just help me open this thing.

ANITA: You can't open a spray bottle, you dork. Haven't you ever painted this thing before?

TINA: No. I used to find it stupid, juvenile. . . . But now I'm seeing it more as a way of mass communication.

ANITA: You really should only be communicating with one person. Isn't that the whole reason for this blowup?

TINA: Maybe . . . OK. Yeah. So what if I didn't call him right after he got home? I mean, is that really any reason to run around on me?

ANITA: For the last time, he didn't run around on you. He took his cousin to her sorority formal dance and *that* was who you saw with him.

TINA: Hence, this whole mass communication of my sincere regrets. Now everyone and their mom will know how I feel.

ANITA: Ugh. Did you really have to use red paint? It's smearing and looks creepily like blood.

TINA: These are Jon's favorite colors. Red, blue, and silver. . . . He tie-dyed a shirt for me in those colors. Ugly as all get out, but the thought was there.

ANITA: And this is the same guy you accuse of running around on you. Does ugly-shirt-giving mean nothing these days?

TINA: There. Done. He'll walk by at exactly 8:19 and see this.

ANITA: And you'll call him?

TINA: And I'll call him.

ANITA: How *do* you tie-dye a shirt silver?

On the Rocks

"Jon. I'm so sorry!"

by Katie

ANN: Maybe I shouldn't do this.

KATE: You have to!

ANN: I know. But something just isn't right about this.

KATE: It was part of the bet, Ann. And you lost fair and square.

ANN: I know. But just because of the dumb bet I have to egg Jon's house?

KATE: You can tell him you're sorry. Write him a note. You know he'll understand.

ANN: OK. This should work. (*She writes "Jon. I'm so sorry!" on the rock*)
KATE: Yeah. That should do it. Now, let's go!

We Did It

(the painting on the rock picture is "We Did It")

by Aaron

JENNY: So. What do you want to paint?
AMANDA: I dunno. Something funny, for sure.
JENNY: Oh, yeah. But it can't be anything that would give us away.
AMANDA: Yeah. I don't want anyone to know we did it.
JENNY: What colors do we have?
AMANDA: Let me check. (*Pause*) Umm. Blue and white.
JENNY: Oh great. All we need is red and we can make it political.
AMANDA: We're not doing that.
JENNY: I know, but at least it could be funny to us.
AMANDA: Does anyone know what your writing looks like?
JENNY: Yeah. A bunch of people at school. Yours?
AMANDA: Yeah, but I've got an idea. What we write, we can write real slow so that the paint runs and no one can tell it was us.
JENNY: But what are we going to write?
AMANDA: *We Did It.*
JENNY: What?
AMANDA: Let's just write *We Did It* and then it's not personal.

These are just four examples of the very first dialogues written by students in the class. The fact that three of these examples are about the same message but with very different themes shows how interesting things can get.

A Short Dialogue Exercise

My playwriting teacher used this exercise to help me write more effective dialogue. I use it throughout the year with my students as an in-class warm-up. At the top of a sheet of lined paper, I ask them to write in the margin a large capital *A* on one line and a large capital *B* on the next line. The *A* and *B* represent two characters and their dialogue with each other.

Next to the *A,* I ask them to write a line that I dictate to them, for example, "Why do you have to do that?" On the next line, next to the *B* I ask them to write the response, "Because." Then they write their own response as *A* on the next line.

An example would be:

A. Why do you have to do that?
B. Because.
A. Don't you know that it annoys me?

Everyone in the class writes a different response. Then they pass their paper to their right. Everyone now has a different paper in front of them and each student reads the dialogue and responds as character *B.*

An example would be:

A. Why do you have to do that?
B. Because.
A. Don't you know it annoys me?
B. No. I didn't know that. But now I do.

They continue passing the paper and writing a responsive line of dialogue.

As their papers make their way around the classroom, remind the students that dialogue is a response to what a character has said before. Sometimes I will have a student write the same line of dialogue on every sheet of paper as it passes. This really sabotages the intent of the exercise. Most of the time I join in the writing and passing of papers because then I can read what is going around and continue to remind the students about dialogue as response. If they know I am reading their responses, they tend to get serious about the exercise, too.

The passing of paper continues until each student gets his original paper back. Then the students are allowed to write two more lines to end the scene. The class then shares their scene by reading it with a partner.

These scenes are never what the original student intended. In some cases, actual characterization emerges because the writers are sensitive to previous character clues in the dialogue. This exercise, besides being a lot of fun, strengthens many playwriting skills. The students get to see how:

- Writing dialogue is a responsive act.
- Characters develop a life of their own.
- Questions help character development like "What does this character want?" and then "What does this character *really* want?"
- When writing a first draft, it is best to go with the flow. Be spontaneous. Improvise.

In Summary

Using the rock pictures has led to some very interesting dialogues. There have been many different interpretations of the same rock picture and message. Some rock pictures are extremely popular and are chosen for scenes more often than others. Some students choose the least chosen picture to challenge and stretch their creativity.

After a student has done one rewrite on their dialogue, I ask them to choreograph the scene with stage directions. I know that this breaks the rules of playwriting and especially those of giving the director too much in the way of character movement, but I want them to experiment with the possibilities of the many ways to paint a rock. I also want to give my performing students a blueprint of how the playwright sees the scene movement when they attempt to do a dramatic read-through of the playwright's work. When the playwrights see their work performed, they realize that many times what they have written in the stage directions has been misunderstood by the performers. It leads to a real awareness of what a playwright should put into stage directions.

Some rock dialogues have grown into short plays when playwrights have added more scenes leading up to the painting of a rock. All of the students like the idea that the act of painting a rock gives energy and movement to their scenes. Somewhere in my future, I can see an evening of rock dialogue scenes with enlarged rock pictures lit and hung overhead. The set would be simple, the props minimal, and the emphasis would be on responsive dialogue. We would play Simon and Garfunkel's "I Am a Rock" and title the evening "Rock My World" or "Rock of Pages."

Seriously, it pains me to realize that I will never know the real story behind the messages on the rocks. But it certainly helps to imagine and write about "Life on the Rocks."

7 Shoes on the Highway*

Have you ever seen a shoe on the side of the road as you drove along? Have you wondered where those individual shoes on the roadside came from? I've seen a sneaker in a ditch, a work boot on top of a guardrail, a baby shoe on the gravel at the side of a culvert, and even one vivid red spiked heel on an entrance ramp. About three years ago, I began taking pictures of these shoes. My daughter, Allison, is also a photographer and has been my sidekick in shoe photography. She rides in the front seat and jumps out to snap a picture of a random shoe on the side of the road. We now have at least eighty different pictures of shoes and our collection continues to grow.

My obsession with shoes on the highway began years ago when I saw my first shoe. I find it one of life's great recurring mysteries. I began to imagine stories about how the shoe got there. My husband and I would see a shoe and off we'd be with a story of how the shoe got there. I began writing a play about shoes on the highway and wondered if these pictures would inspire my young playwrights as well.

I began to collect these photographs to use them for a playwriting exercise. Using a visual cue for writing a play—like photos of random

* This chapter is based on an article that was first printed in the Educational Theatre Association's publication *Teaching Theatre* (2003).

shoes—can be challenging and thought provoking. I'm sure that the visual cue of a glass unicorn inspired Tennessee Williams for "The Glass Menagerie" or that the sights and sounds of small-town America helped Thornton Wilder create "Our Town." Symbolic objects laden with meaning can be found in any play you pick up. I found these singular shoes curious and hoped that my class of playwrights would find them just as provocative in the creation of their plays.

I brought in some of our photographs. I spread them out on a table. The reaction of the students as they walked into the room and saw the pictures was something I wish you could have seen. They were drawn to the pictures, asking questions about where and when we had found them.

I asked my class to take a closer look at a few of these pictures and brainstorm about how they thought the shoe got there. Then, through character creation, imaginative storytelling, and strong conflicting objectives, they would write a ten-minute play about how the shoe got there. At some time during the play, the shoe would end up on the highway. As a final project, the plays would be presented in a dramatic reading session in our Black Box Theatre.

The "Shoes on the Highway" project was a three- to four-week unit that I taught to my eleventh- and twelfth-grade playwriting class. There were fourteen students in the class and the project took about fifteen to twenty class periods, with forty-five minutes of meeting time per class. The unit could also be taught to an Acting One class or an English class. The students need to be able to look at the picture of the shoe and imagine who would have worn the shoe, what kind of person would have thrown it onto the highway, and what event or conflict would have caused the shoe to end up on the side of the road. In other words, the students need to be able to visualize, imagine, and write.

I chose three of my shoe pictures to concentrate on with the class: a work boot in the snow, a tennis shoe in a ditch, and a child's shoe on a patch of gravel. I chose these photos because I thought it would be easy for the students to imagine the conflict or the character in relation to these pictures. The pictures themselves were sharp and clear and the roadside was visible in each picture.

Before I showed them the first picture, we talked about seeing shoes on the side of the road.

"How many of you have seen a shoe on the highway or the side of a road?"

Every student had seen at least one shoe.

"What type of shoe was it?"

Tennis shoe, high heel, hiking boot.

"Specifically, where did you see the shoe?"

On ramps, country roads, parking lots, and even on the island that divides the highway.

"How do you think they got there?"

They talked a bit about what might have happened to result in a shoe being thrown out a car window or falling off of a garbage truck. The discussion and brainstorming about possible scenarios got more imaginative the more we talked.

"What if a kid didn't like the shoes his mom or dad bought him and chucked them out the window?"

"What if the shoes were an expensive present from an ex-spouse and the parent, in a fit of anger, knowing the ex was trying to buy the love of her children, threw them out the window?"

"What if there was a tragic car accident and someone's shoe was left behind?"

During the discussion, there was no shortage of ideas.

Then I showed them the picture of a work boot in the snow. I asked them to write a few sentences on a sheet of paper about the work boot and how it got there. We did the same thing with the other two pictures, a tennis shoe in a ditch at the side of the road and a child's shoe on a patch of gravel. We then shared our ideas aloud in a class discussion. We talked about character, story line, and possible conflicts.

For example, one student imagined that the tennis shoe in a ditch had been left behind after a car accident. She suggested a story about how a girl had been driving the family car too fast after an argument with her friend and had flipped the car over in the ditch. She wanted to start the play with the friend finding the shoe as she visits the highway to lay some flowers there in remembrance of her friend.

Another student took the picture of the child's shoe and suggested that a three-year-old had flung it out the window.

"What was the driver doing?"

"The mom was busy trying to stop an argument between her kids in the car. She didn't notice that her little kid had thrown the shoe out an open window when the car was traveling at a high speed."

"Would the mom stop the car to go back for the shoe?"

"I don't know."

"That's something to think about."

The next step was to work on a play as an entire class. I limited the number of characters in the play to four or five so that the playwrights could concentrate on developing them. We chose one of the three pictures. The picture of the child's shoe was their favorite. As a class, we wrote up a playwriting grid on the board (see the Appendix, page 122). I don't require the use of this grid with every playwriting assignment because it sometimes limits the creative flow of playwriting. But, for some playwriting assignments, I find that it gives the young playwrights a comfortable structure on which to build their story. The grid consists of a list of such terms as:

- exposition
- strong conflicting objectives
- initial incident
- complications
- crisis
- climax
- falling action and conflict resolution

These terms were all written on the board. The class then decided, through discussion, on a few sentences or even key words and phrases that fit the categories.

For example, next to exposition we listed the characters and a short description of what was happening "At Rise." We also listed a few traits for each character. The major conflict was a few sentences in length, as was the initial incident. This process did not happen smoothly as each student had different ideas as to what they wanted written down. When the class could not agree, I stepped in and made a decision.

The finished grid looked something like this when it was finished:

Playwriting Grid

Exposition: Mrs. Trumble (a perfectionist) is driving down the highway. Her children, Tim (13, shy and sensitive) Taryn (10, loud and bossy), and Troy (3) are in the car. A policeman appears at the end of the play.

Strong, conflicting objectives: They are late for a doctor's appointment. Tim and Taryn are arguing about a girl that Taryn says is

Tim's girlfriend. Mrs. Trumble is trying to get to the doctor's appointment and settle the argument. The baby, Troy, is trying to untie the shoelaces on his shoes.

Initial incident: Taryn starts to tease Tim about his "girlfriend."

Complications: Traffic increases; Tim denies knowing the girl and gets angry; Taryn persists in giving examples of times she's seen him walking with her; Mrs. Trumble tries to intervene by suggesting that they play the "Quiet" game; Troy cries in frustration; Tim unties Troy's shoe.

Crisis: Troy's shoe goes out the window; the kids try to tell their Mom about the shoe but she is ranting about the traffic and the noise.

Climax: Siren is heard. Policeman pulls car over.

Falling action and conflict resolution: The policeman does not give her a ticket but returns Troy's shoe. Mrs. Trumble apologizes and says she didn't see the shoe go out the window because of the arguing and noise. Policeman suggests that they play the "Quiet" game.

With the completed grid as a guide, I asked the students to write up the first three pages of a ten-minute play. Students wrote their own scene. The information on the grid and the character descriptions had to be used as the basis for the three-minute scene. The scene must begin to show what part the shoe plays in the conflict and how it could end up on the highway. After all, the point of the scene is to answer the question, "How did the shoe end up on the highway?"

I gave this three-page scene creation as a homework assignment. The writing of the three-minute scene is only a preparation for a longer assignment. Modeling the process we used for the picture of the child's shoe helps the students write a ten-minute play after choosing their own shoe picture to inspire them. There will be more on that process later.

During the next few classes, we read all of the three-minute scenes out loud. It is very important for the young playwright to hear their scenes. A discussion followed each reading as the playwright critiqued the scene in response to the question, "What did you hear?" We use this question with every read-through and it prompts the playwright to listen for dialogue that doesn't sound natural. The rest of the class offered suggestions about clarification of objectives, characterization, and story line. The class also critiqued the dialogue if some word or phrase sounded out of place. This process is used, not just for these plays, but for every play written in class during the semester. I let the class finish with their critique and then I gave my suggestions.

If your class is large, you may want to undertake the critiquing process in small groups. After we read and discussed all of the three-minute scenes, the students were ready for the next step of choosing a new picture, modeling the process they just used, and writing a ten-minute play.

Pictures of Shoes on the Highway

I brought out all of my shoe pictures (fifteen to twenty) and passed them around the class. There were pictures of a sandal in the snow, a sneaker hanging on high-tension wires, a red dress shoe near a storm drain, and a large black boot surrounded by old pop cans. (These pictures can be found in the Appendix on pages 94–110 and on the Heinemann website, www.heinemann.com, and can be reproduced for your writing class.)

To write the ten-minute play, the students used the same process that we used to write the shorter, three-minute scene: the construction of a playwriting grid. There are a few other requirements for this ten-minute play. The play had to address the question of how the shoe got there. I asked them to limit the number of characters in their play to three or four and to remember to give them strong, conflicting objectives. The play did not have to take place in a car or on the highway, but it could be set anywhere as long as they answered the pivotal question about how the shoe got on the highway.

Writing a ten-minute play presents its own challenges. An excellent article to use as a guide is "10 Tools for Writing 10-Minute Plays" by Gary Garrison (*Dramatics* 2002). This humorous article has some serious advice on how to tackle this incredible, immediate art form made famous by the Actors Theatre Louisville. *Perfect Ten* (Garrison 2001) is another resource that I use with my playwriting class. It is also filled with excellent examples and advice.

The students had a week to finish the ten-minute play. When all the students finished their first draft, we spent the next three classes reading each ten-minute play out loud and critiquing it. I gave my students one rewrite before I graded the play. I tell my students that after one rewrite and a grade from me they shouldn't think the play is done. If a play is to make it from page to stage, many, many rewrites are necessary.

The following plays were written by my students. These plays had only two rewrites and they are still "in process" but it is helpful and interesting to see the efforts of these young playwrights and their response to this assignment.

The first play was written by Jessie. I thought it had a distinctly absurdist quality to it. Her play was performed during our lunchtime play readings. It used minimalist blocking and some basic lighting. Even during its first reading, the play had a very poignant quality to it.

Monuments

by Jessie

Characters

ALEX Short for Alexandria, a 15-year-old girl. She's Christian, and should be wearing a Christian school uniform. She should look pretty beat up, clothes should be torn, dirty, her face should be dirty, and hair messed up. She should look tired and depressed, as well. She's very sad.
WOMAN A mysterious woman, dressed all in black, no definable personality. Her face should be hidden by a hood.
MAN: A mysterious man, dressed all in black, no definable personality. A hood should hide his face.

Setting: Alex's dream, and in the dream the setting is a highway. There are cars, but the cars don't move; the dream is a suspension of reality. The highway has two lanes going one way, one lane going the other. There is a grassy median. A pair of black, combat boots is in this median; they look pretty beaten up. There is a car wreck on the one-lane road; a few cop cars and an ambulance are there. A backdrop could serve to provide this setting.

At Rise: ALEX *is standing in the middle of the two-lane road, center stage.* WOMAN *is downstage right,* MAN *is center stage left. Both are wearing all black, faces hidden by hoods, turned away from* ALEX. ALEX *looks around slowly, sees the combat boots. She stares at them for a few moments and walks toward them. There's a flash of light, and she's by* WOMAN.

WOMAN: I can curl my tongue. (*She demonstrates*) Can you?

ALEX: No. I mean, who cares? I've never been able to, even if I wanted to.

WOMAN: All you need is practice. See, like this. (*She demonstrates again. Alex tries, unsuccessfully*) No, you have to suck in air a little more. (*She does it again, as does Alex, again unsuccessfully*)

ALEX: No, I still can't do it. It doesn't really matter. I don't want to try anymore.

WOMAN: It's just practice.

ALEX: Actually, I read somewhere that it's a certain muscle in their tongue that some people are born without . . . and that's why they can't do it.

(*Beat*)

I was born without it. I would know. I practiced when I was a kid.

(*Pause*)

Now that I think about it, I could never raise one eyebrow, either.

WOMAN: I'm sure all that you needed was practice.

ALEX: No, nothing would have helped. (*There's another flash of light*)

WOMAN: Did you know that we only use 10 percent of our brains?

ALEX: Yes.

(*Pause*)

But I'd hate to think that a . . . cheerleader is as smart as me.

WOMAN: (*Nods*) Or that a psycho thinks the same way we do.

ALEX: (*Angry*) No, their brains are different. They couldn't *possibly* be like us. Some lobe or another. (*She walks to Man*) These cars . . . they're frozen! Where are we?

MAN: Some interstate. (*Alex looks surprised*)

ALEX: You . . . don't see? (*Alex gestures toward the cars*)
MAN: I don't care. I'm just alone and lost . . .
ALEX: That's too bad. What time is it?
MAN: (*Looks at his watch*) 10 P.M.
ALEX: That's the east over there right?
MAN: Yes.
ALEX: The sun's rising at 10 P.M.?
MAN: My watch must be broken.

ALEX *sits at the side of the road.*

ALEX: My watch broke when I was little. Actually, my cousin accidentally broke it. (*Man grunts*) It was my favorite . . . it had Mickey Mouse on it; the hands were his gloves you know? (*Alex sighs*) Things are so different now.

WOMAN *comes over.*

WOMAN: Everything turns out okay in the end.
ALEX: Not this time.
MAN: Why not?
ALEX: I really messed up.
MAN: That's your car?
ALEX: (*Nods*) I borrowed it from my parents.
WOMAN: Borrowed?
ALEX: I would have given it back eventually . . .
MAN: And those . . . your shoes?
ALEX: Kind of . . . they were my cousin's. (*Flash of light*) My parents loved that car.
WOMAN: Leather interior.
MAN: Fully loaded.
ALEX: Gone.
WOMAN: Things pick up.
MAN: (*Eagerly*) They can't get worse.
ALEX: I don't agree.
WOMAN: But . . . why not?
MAN: (*To Woman*) Shh! (*He whispers to Woman*) The funeral's tomorrow, remember?
ALEX: Yep. At 7 A.M.
WOMAN: Sunrise.
ALEX: The way it should be.

MAN: What actually happened?

ALEX: I just wanted to get away from it all . . . (*She looks toward the boots*) Get rid of it all.

WOMAN: (*Pause*) . . . and before that?

ALEX: She was murdered . . . (*Starts crying*) Cops can't even figure out who did it. (*Cries harder*) I was just trying to forget . . .

WOMAN: (*Understanding*) By leaving . . .

MAN: But the shoes reminded you of her?

ALEX: So I was going to leave them here. It's not like they can bring her back.

WOMAN: And they can't show you who did it.

ALEX: (*Frustrated*) That doesn't matter—she's gone!

WOMAN: What about justice?

ALEX: It doesn't even mean anything anymore. Revenge won't bring her back, neither will justice, neither will God.

MAN: She's with Him now.

WOMAN: He'll bring her back to you when she's ready.

ALEX: I'd sell my soul to have her back. (*Flash of light*) She loved those shoes. Look at them now.

WOMAN: (*Looks toward wreck*) Your parents loved that car.

MAN: Look at it now . . . (*Beat. Man looks like he's searching for something to say*) But God does still love you.

ALEX: Look at me now. (*Another flash*)

WOMAN *walks to center stage, standing, and hovers over the shoes.*

MAN *follows and does the same thing.* ALEX *follows* MAN *and kneels by the shoes.*

WOMAN: They're not in too bad of shape . . .

MAN: A little polish—

WOMAN: A little glue . . .

MAN: Didn't they use to pinch her feet a little?

ALEX: Yea, they were so old . . .

WOMAN: Too small for her.

ALEX: Sole was wearing down. (*Beat*) But she could still never part with them.

WOMAN *picks up the combat boots, looks at them for a few moments, and kneels.*

She offers them to ALEX.

ALEX: No. They belong here . . .

MAN: But don't you want to return them? (*Alex shakes her head. Woman stands*)
You're probably right.

WOMAN: (*Nods*) Yes, she's better without them if they hurt.

ALEX: She won't find them here.

MAN: She won't look for them.

WOMAN: She can't look for them.

ALEX: She's gone . . .

MAN: (*Firmly*) But she's in heaven.

WOMAN: She's free now.

MAN: From pain . . .

WOMAN: Worries . . .

ALEX: Sorrow . . . ? (*Small flash*)
Am . . . am I free too?

MAN: (*Man looks away sadly, then turns back to Alex and nods*)
Yes . . . just a few moments ago.

WOMAN: Don't worry . . .

ALEX: (*Cries softly as she looks back toward wreck*) But look what I've done . . .

MAN: You won't have to explain it . . .

WOMAN: They can't yell at you . . .

ALEX: You're right. And I can tell Ayda not to worry about her shoes anymore.

MAN: Exactly.

WOMAN: It'll be nice to see her again. (*She offers the shoes to Alex again, who declines again*)

WOMAN: You're sure?

MAN: She is.

ALEX: I have to be getting back now.

MAN: Remember that He is with you.

ALEX: How could I possibly forget?

She walks back toward wreck. She looks back toward MAN *and* WOMAN. *There's a flash and* ALEX *disappears.*

MAN: Nice girl.

WOMAN: Wrecked shoes. Should we throw them away?

MAN: I think she wanted us to leave them here.
WOMAN: They'll still be thrown away.
MAN: Then we won't have to be bothered.
WOMAN: So we'll just leave them alone.
MAN: Alone right here.
WOMAN: Here on the highway.
The End

This next play is by Jeffrey. I thought the opening was surrealistic and unique. The shoes fall from a bridge down to a homeless person below. Jeffrey is an incredible photographer and the visual nature of the plays he wrote was marvelous!

Shoes from Above

by Jeffrey

Characters

GABRIELA Eleven-year-old girl, insightful, energetic.
SHIRLEY TEMPLE A homeless woman who lives under a highway bridge, very quiet.
LADY forty years old
OFFICER A male police officer with a deep voice.

Setting: Under a highway bridge (scene I). A twelve-year-old kid's room (scene II).

Time: 2003

At Rise: *Stage is completely dark except for a spotlight (center stage). A pair of shoes falls from above into the spotlight.*

Car traffic is heard and after shoes fall into spotlight, SHIRLEY walks onstage and picks them up and looks at them then looks around.

SHIRLEY: Oh Lord! Why would somebody throw their shoes down here? Or were they thrown at me? I can't keep these, these are somebody's and that somebody isn't me. (*Shirley reaches in shoe, pulls out piece of paper, and begins to read it*)

Dear Mrs, These were my shoes. I lost them by this bridge a few years ago. I don't know who you are but I figured you get real lonely down here. I figured you might be a little hungry so I put some crackers and candy in the shoes for you. If you can put the shoes up by the bridge near the bike path, I can get them and write back to you. Love, Gabriela.

SHIRLEY *sits down and begins vigorously looking through all of her stuff.*

SHIRLEY: I need a pen! I need a pen! Ah ha!

Stands up and holds pen up high. SHIRLEY *begins to write on shoe but realizes pen doesn't work.*

SHIRLEY: I've got a pen. I've got the shoes to write on, but I can't write back to this girl . . . Gabriela. Who am I kidding? I don't even remember how to write! (*Shirley sits back down. Begins to read the message on the shoe to herself*) Maybe I can talk to her if I wait by the bike path. (*Shirley walks stage left and sits on a bench then lies down and goes to sleep. Dim to blackout*)

GABRIELA: (*Sneaks onstage then takes the shoes. Leaves the stage. She is heard offstage*) Dear Mrs, What is your name? I hope you like the crackers, those were always my favorite. I realized you might have needed a pen to write me back so I put one in the shoes. I also put in some more crackers. What do you do all day? Love, Gabriela.

Stage lights dim on. Shoes fall from above stage to center stage.

SHIRLEY: (*Wakes up when hears shoes. Shirley walks over to shoes*) Where are these coming from: (*Picks up shoes, takes out note and reads the message to herself*) My name? . . . I . . . I don't really remember . . . oh wait . . . I remember the name Shirley . . . Shirley Teh . . . Teh . . . Temple . . . Shirley Temple. I remember now. I better write this down before I forget. (*She begins to write on the shoe*) I am Shirley Temple. What do I do all day? Hmmm . . . I look for jobs but nobody wants me. I think . . . I think about what it'd be like to be on top of the bridge where everyone else is, where you probably throw the shoes from. Love Shirley (*She folds the note and puts it back in the shoe*)

OFFICER: (*Walks onstage toward Shirley*) Hi, I'm Officer Dufrain and you are?

SHIRLEY: I'm Shirley, Shirley Temple.

OFFICER: (*He chuckles, then he puts his hand on her back and they begin to walk toward offstage*) I'm sure you are. Look, we really can't have you living here Mrs. Uh . . . Temple. I'll be back around six o'clock and you sure as hell better have all your crap ready to go to the homeless shelter. I'm sure it won't take you long, Mrs. Temple. (*He laughs*)

SHIRLEY: (*Stops abruptly and turns the other way*) But Officer, I can't. See my mother uh . . . Gabriela, was gonna visit me tomorrow and she's gonna come visit me here, under this bridge.

OFFICER: Was what I said not clear Mrs. Temple? Oh, and Mrs. Temple, let's say you're not ready to go when I come back later, you will be taken into custody! (*Turns and walks offstage*)

SHIRLEY: (*She sits down and takes out the food and begins to eat*) I better put these shoes by the path before I fall asleep. (*Walks to bench, puts shoes down and goes to sleep. Dim to blackout and the shoes are taken offstage. Spotlight shines on Shirley and she frantically wakes up and realizes the shoes are gone*)

The shoes! The shoes! I need these shoes! (*Shoes fall onto stage and she looks up to see where they came from but is blinded by the spotlight, also car traffic is heard*)

During the next part of the play, Gabriela invites Shirley, via the note in the shoes, to her house for dinner. She decides to wear the shoes from above to the dinner. When she gets to the house she learns from the lady in the house that the little girl has been dead for years. She died in an accident that took place under the bridge.

The next play was written by Anna and it involves a dream, too. The main character has a nagging dream and when she tries to explain it to her friend, she has a hard time making her understand how haunting this particular dream is to her.

I Had a Dream Last Night

by Anna

Characters

HANNAH Sixteen years old, quiet but friendly. Throughout this entire scene she is shaken and speaks sometimes slowly and sometimes frantically.

JACKIE She is Hannah's good friend and bus buddy. She is the same age as Hannah but acts a little older. She is often sarcastic but is also very caring. She starts out the scene annoyed and sarcastic but grows more and more sympathetic to Hannah as the play progresses.

Setting: A crowded public bus in New York City

Time: Present day

At Rise: *There are a few benches set up representing a bus. There doesn't need to be people on the benches.* JACKIE *is sitting on one of the benches staring out the "window." Lights are up on the bus but the rest of the stage is dark. There could also be bus noises playing. Throughout the whole play the characters should act as if they are on a crowded bus, being shook around and jostled by people.*

At Rise: HANNAH *enters the "bus" and acts out handing money to the driver. She makes her way clumsily to* JACKIE'S *seat and sits down.* HANNAH *is very distracted and keeps looking over* JACKIE *out the window.*

JACKIE: Hey!

HANNAH: Hi.

JACKIE: Did you find that book I was talking about? The one about the Russian Revolution?

HANNAH: What? Oh, no . . .

JACKIE: But you said you would find that! We need that for the paper—how're we supposed to write it now?

HANNAH: Um, I dunno, I brought *these* books.

JACKIE: Yeah, but those don't have anything about the Russian Revolution in them, which is why I called you about that book last night, 'cause it was kinda important Hannah, now what—

HANNAH: Can I switch seats with you?

JACKIE: What? Why? Are you even listening to what I'm saying?

HANNAH: Yeah, yeah, the Russians, I'm really sorry . . . but can you . . . switch?

JACKIE: Why? You're just gonna have to get off in a couple minutes anyway since the library's on this route and you forgot to get the book. Ugh, now I'm gonna have to do all the computer stuff all by myself. . . .

HANNAH: Please, Jackie, switch? I, um, really, *really*, want to look out the window.

JACKIE: . . . Ok . . . ?

HANNAH clumsily climbs over JACKIE so she is next to the window and stares out of it. She barely looks away from it for the remainder of the scene.

JACKIE: What are you looking for?

HANNAH: Nothing.

JACKIE: Nothing! Oh you're looking for nothing! That's gonna be kinda hard to find . . . how 'bout you look for that Russian book instead, you might have more luck with that.

HANNAH: No . . . Jackie!

JACKIE: What? What is going on with you, Hannah? You definitely weren't like this when I called last night.

HANNAH: That's because it hadn't happened yet. When you called.

JACKIE: What? (*Jackie becomes very concerned*) Oh my God, are you OK? Did something happen last night? Did someone . . .

HANNAH: No, no, nothing like that.

JACKIE: Then what? Hey, maybe if you tell me what's wrong I could help you look for your . . . nothing.

HANNAH: I had a dream last night.

JACKIE: *This* is the problem? Was it about Australian football players in muumuus again? Handicapped people sliding down escalators?

HANNAH: No.

JACKIE: Then what? Hannah—

HANNAH: Jackie, do you ever notice the shoes in the streets?

JACKIE: What shoes?

HANNAH: They're everywhere. I mean it's like . . . air. It's everywhere but you never see it. Shoes are everywhere.

JACKIE: (*Jackie gives Hannah an "are-you-insane?" look which Hannah does not see. Jackie looks around the bus skeptically*) Um, no? I mean I've got some shoes on, so do you, that kid's got some, that guy—oh no, gross, well that kid does, but they're definitely not everywhere—

HANNAH: Shoes on the streets. On the highways. By the sides of the roads . . .

JACKIE: Oh OK . . . is this the nothing we're looking for?

HANNAH: I had a dream last night.

JACKIE: So I heard. (*Pause*) Would you like to *tell* me about it?

HANNAH: (*Hannah speaks haltingly*) I was in a plane and . . . I had to fly it for some reason.

JACKIE: Here we go . . .

HANNAH: I think the pilots had died. My great-aunt was on the plane too, the one who . . . you know, went all Sylvia Plath, and she was talking to my boyfriend from preschool—

JACKIE: Wait, wait, wait, who was your preschool boyfriend? Was it, whatshisface, that Mikey kid?

HANNAH: (*Hannah does not hear what Jackie says. As Hannah continues, she becomes more and more distraught, bordering on tears*) Yeah, yeah, Mikey. He was still in preschool, just the same. I had to fly the plane but we were eating caramel apples and I got caramel all over the panel and the buttons were sticking. So the plane started to crash, just nosedive and we're racing past streets, 113th . . . 99th . . . 51st . . . 17th . . . 2nd . . . Houston . . . Canal . . . We're headed for the World Trade Center.

JACKIE *looks concerned and puts her hand on* HANNAH's *shoulder.*

HANNAH: Everyone was so scared. But just as we're about to hit I get a button clean and we pull up. But the button made us go fast, really fast but . . . I could see everything going by. Roosevelt's hospital, and then our first apartment, and then the swing set at Central Park . . . where I broke my leg and that ice cream place we used to hang out and the restaurant I had my first date at, at . . .

JACKIE: Ollie's.

HANNAH: Yeah. I mean, I knew all the places and even though it was a big blur—I knew each one. And if the plane slowed down or sped up we would die but what we had to do was land and then it would be OK. So, I'm searching out the window through all the blur of everything I know and I have this periscope thing to zoom in on the places to find somewhere to land so it'll be OK. And everyone on the plane is screaming and ripping out their fingernails trying to open the windows and jump out. And then all of a sudden my periscope narrows in on something and there's this loud *shrieking* alarm and the plane is going so fast I can't breathe and I look what we're zooming in on and . . . and it's pair of shoes. Just sitting on a street, all torn up, with this glow around them.

(*Pause*)

JACKIE: Shoes?

HANNAH: And I woke up, just shot up and I still couldn't breathe but . . . I was so scared.

JACKIE: Of the shoes?

HANNAH: I had *never* seen them before.

JACKIE: Ok, um—

HANNAH: (*Hannah now speaks very fast*) *Never.* It was like . . . I mean you know what a dream is right? It's just a crazy collage of everything you've seen before over the last however many years of your life. You never make new things in your dreams because your eyes are closed and the visual-eye part of your brain is turned off.

JACKIE: So—

HANNAH: But the shoes. I had never seen them before. I mean, I might have seen those specific shoes, like the visuals might have been the same but the other senses that went with it, I had never ever *felt* that before. And they were all torn and . . . and that glow . . . it was like I was seeing them for the first time.

JACKIE: But you just said you *can't* see new things in dreams.

HANNAH: But I did. It felt so . . . foreign. Like someone had stuck some cold metal probe into my brain and it didn't belong there at all. It wasn't mine.

JACKIE: Someone's sticking shoes in your head?

HANNAH: I don't know but . . . I've got to find them.

JACKIE *and* HANNAH *are now both staring out the window*

JACKIE: Maybe there are some shoes out there that we go by every day and you didn't know you knew them but they just kinda slipped into your brain.

HANNAH: I had never seen those shoes before. I had never felt anything like that. And I've been looking the whole time and I *don't see any shoes.*

JACKIE: Well, what's gonna happen when you find them?

HANNAH: I don't know but . . . as stupid and clichéd as it all sounds, it just feels like my entire life rests upon these shoes! And I just . . . need to find them. (*Jackie looks away from the window but you can tell she's really scared*)

JACKIE: This is stupid, this is so stupid. You just had a stupid dream and it probably freaked you out but that doesn't mean it's suddenly your entire life, or, or . . .

HANNAH: Those shoes did not belong there.

JACKIE: I know.

HANNAH: Those shoes . . . I—I don't know what they mean. I don't know! Like, if I still remembered how to pray I would be down on my *knees* because I'm . . . pretty freaked out. (*The bus slows and they jerk forward and finally look away from the window and at each other*)

JACKIE: Look, here's the library. Try to find that book and I'll do the computer stuff as soon as I can and come find you . . . maybe you'll have calmed down by then.

HANNAH: I had never seen those shoes before.

JACKIE: I know. Bye.

HANNAH *gets up and squeezes off the bus. Lights go down on the bus and there is a spotlight up on* HANNAH. *There are bus squealing noises as the bus pulls away.* HANNAH *starts to walk off then freezes and looks down.*

HANNAH: Oh, my God. They were my shoes? But—they were my shoes!

HANNAH *turns around and starts running to the opposite side of the stage, after the bus. The spotlight follows* HANNAH.

HANNAH: Jackie! Th-those were my shoes lying in the street!

She runs off stage as she says the last line.

HANNAH: They were my—

There is a loud crash and thud and the sound of car brakes squealing. The lights fade.

The "Shoes on the Highway" plays were given a dramatic reading by my theatre students at a lunchtime event in our Black Box Theatre. I cast the plays with the theatre students from Acting One, Two, and Advanced Acting classes. You can also run tryouts for these dramatic readings or ask for volunteers from the drama students at your school. The playwriting class was required to be in attendance to hear the audience's reaction to their plays. The audience, which packed the Black Box, also helped to critique the plays by answering a short questionnaire about the plays. This questionnaire can be found in the Appendix, page 120. The questions the audience are asked are:

- Does the dialogue sound believable? Is there any dialogue that doesn't sound natural?
- Are the characters interesting and well-defined?
- What is the conflict?
- Is the story line easy to follow?
- What was you favorite part? . . . your least favorite part?

After this performance, the playwrights had another week to read through the comments and rewrite their plays. Then they turned them in for a final grade. I tried to impress upon them that in the real world of playwriting, a few more performances would give them more opportunities to rewrite and perfect their plays. Because of time constraints, we only had one dramatic read-through.

Through the years, I have been amazed at the creativity of the classes' ten-minute plays! They range from the extremely sober to the completely wacky to absurdist and futuristic. "Monuments," which appears earlier in the chapter, spoke of a teenager who was determined to leave one of her friend's shoes at the spot where she was killed in a car accident. Two spirits oversee the process and there is a surprise twist with the main character at the end of the play. Another student, Georgia, wrote a play called "Running Black" based on the picture of the black boots on the railroad tracks picture. "Bad Trip," "Common Soles," "Baby Shoes," and "Worn In. Worn Out" all have the common thread of shoes being flung out the window of a car. The characters that do the flinging are different and unique, as are the reasons for the shoes ending up on the highway. "Midnight" is about the deceased father and grandfather of three female characters. His profession was a shoemaker. "At Burger King. In the Future" is a play about a robot that goes crazy when his blind date doesn't work out and he flings his shoes out the door at a Burger King. "The Truth About Love" is about a group of people who are about two inches in height. They find a shoe and want to use it as a home. These plays are absurdist and fantastical plays about love and, what else, shoes.

I used shoes as a visual cue because they provoked me to think. Why was there only one shoe? How did the shoe get on the side of the road? What does a lonely shoe say about our society where everything is disposable? Is the shoe a metaphor for something else? Growing old? Being alone? I've tried to explore these questions by writing a play called "Shoes on the Highway."

I went through the same process that I took my students through. The cast of middle school students performed this play at my school. I rewrote as they rehearsed and the play got better and better. The play received a wonderful response from the audience. This past summer, the play won third place in the Nantucket Short Play Contest and received staged readings there October 2004. I am still doing rewrites. My students know that I share this journey with them as a fellow playwright.

I've shared this idea of shoes on the highway with students, parents, and friends, and everyone has a story to tell about the shoes they've seen along the roadside. They have even thought about stopping their cars and taking a picture to add to my growing collection!

One parent shared a real-life drama with me that involved some kids tossing a pair of shoes at a barefoot, homeless man in downtown Cleveland. The man, who was tired and hungry, just walked past the shoes and there they remained, on the roadside. What a potential character to use for a play! I've learned that there's a story for every shoe on the highway. And "story" and "character" are what playwriting is all about.

Appendix: Photographs

YOUR HELP!

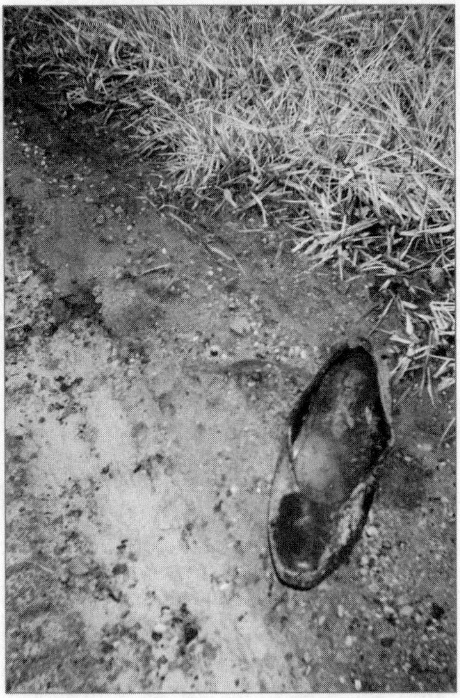

JON.
I'M SO SORRY!

ben,
i miss u
already

and
you're
amazing!

THANX
MOM
&
DAD

LONG
LIVE
SUMMER

GOOD
LUCK
MOM

Thank
You Rachel

CHURCH
OF
SIN
THE FEVE
8PM FRI

LEARN
ABOUT
THE DRAFT
FRI FEB 27
7:30 CRAIG

Appendix: Forms

Guide for Writing Significant Object Monologue

Name ____

Describe the object:

____

____

____

Ideas to keep in mind when writing the monologue:

- Use first person.
- Don't tell us too much too soon.
- The monologue should have a beginning, a middle, and an end.
- The beginning should grab the audience's attention.
- Keep it simple. The audience should be able to follow your story easily.
- It should only be one page in length/double-spaced.

Use this space to write up the rough draft and then retype it and save it on your computer or disk. You will hand in your rough draft as well as your good copy.

Significant Object Monologue

Beginning

____

____

____

____

____

____

____

____

____

Middle

End

The monologue is due ______________________________

You will be reading your monologue out loud in front of the class.

Questions About Clothing for "Wear the Character"

1. When you go home to relax, what clothes do you change into?

2. What are your favorite casual clothes?

3. How do you feel when you wear these clothes?

4. Describe your dressiest outfit.

5. Where and when do you wear these clothes?

6. How do you feel when you wear these clothes?

7. Tell me a story about a time when you got all dressed up *or* tell me a story about a time when you bought a new outfit.

Favorite Song Essay

Name ____

Choose a song that takes you to a different time and place in your mind every time you hear it. This song should have significant meaning to you. Please answer the following questions in essay form on this sheet of paper. Use the back of the sheet, too.

- Why is this one of your favorite songs? Be specific.

- Where and when did you hear the song for the first time?

- What memories does this song bring to mind?

- Is there a particular phrase or part of a lyric that really resonates with you? Include these phrases at the end of your essay.

Audience Critique

Please answer the following questions about the dramatic reading. Your reactions will help guide the playwright in making changes to the script.

Does the dialogue sound believable? Is there any dialogue that doesn't sound natural? Give examples.

Are the characters interesting and well-defined?

What is the conflict?

Is the story line easy to follow? Can you summarize the play in two or three sentences?

What was you favorite part?

Your least favorite part?

Juxtaposition

Take a look at the picture.
Brainstorm by answering the following questions:

- How did that object get there?

- Who put it there? Why did they put it there?

- In what ways are these objects similar? Dissimilar?

- Can you figure out a relationship between the objects?

Playwriting Grid

Name ______________________________

Assignment ______________________________

Write a few sentences or even key words and phrases about your play that fit the categories.

- Exposition

- Strong, conflicting objectives

- Initial incident

- Complications

- Crisis

- Climax

- Falling action/conflict resolution